T0120830

A DUET OF CHRIST AND CHURCH

An Interpretation & Commentary on Song of Songs

BISHOP DR. IMRAN BHATTI

WestBow Press books may be ordered through booksellers or by contacting:

WestBow Press
A Division of Thomas Nelson & Zondervan
1663 Liberty Drive
Bloomington, IN 47403
www.westbowpress.com
844-714-3454

Scripture taken from the World English Bible.

ISBN: 978-1-6642-4373-6 (sc)
ISBN: 978-1-6642-4372-9 (e)

Library of Congress Control Number: 2021917762

Print information available on the last page.

WestBow Press rev. date: 11/05/2021

CONTENTS

INTRODUCTION

Song of Songs is a book which is difficult to understand and many people misunderstand the scriptures given within it. This is a small book with big revelations. Some people take it as a book which talks about Solomon's love for a maid. Some think it is a love story of a shepherd boy who was in love with a beautiful girl, but Solomon took that girl forcefully. So there are different kinds of thoughts about this book.

The Bible is not just a collection of books which contains love stories of individuals. It is a love story of God and His people from cover to cover. In this way, if we take Song of Songs as only a love story of King Solomon, it means we doubt the divinity of the Bible. If the Bible is the Word of God then the Song of Songs, being part of the Bible, must be the Word of God as well. Therefore, this whole book, Song of Songs, is a deeper revelation of the love God has for the church (His bride).

I have taken each and every verse in this book as a love song between God and His church. You will be amazed how deep the love of God is for us individually, and as a church. In these verses you will find hidden revelations about worship. We are taught how we can worship God. When we worship, God reveals secrets of the present, past and future. In this book you will find how God revealed not only His love but His future plans as well.

I pray and hope that this book may become a blessing for you and take you to new heights of understanding the Bible.

Bishop Dr. Imran Bhatti

FOREWORD

If there is one book of the Bible that has frustrated theologians over the centuries, it is the *Song of Solomon.* Just eight chapters long, its symbolism as well as quasi-erotic language has intimidated commentators on God's Holy Word. Some, like John Calvin, failed to even write a sentence about this book when they produced their commentaries during the Reformation. Others have tried to dismiss it as being simply "a love poem". *A Duet of Christ and Church* shines a long overdue light on what may be the most insightful book of the Old Testament.

Rt. Rev. Dr. Imran Bhatti has brought a freshness to this controversial book of the Bible. Rather than simply dismissing it or lightly brushing over it, he charges deep into the very heart of *Song of Solomon.* Line by line, he dissects its hidden meanings.

Dr. Bhatti brings his unique hermeneutical approach to Song of Solomon. He combines new scholarship with his background as a Pakistani Christian. He tells the long-forgotten story which shows the unique relationship between God and his people. He explores the unique love that God has for his people. He shows us the very presence of Jesus Christ amidst of the love story.

It is a love story. It is greater than any human love story. It expresses deep intimacy, yet rejects the erotic for a much greater agape love that only God can give to his people.

The bride is the church; the bridegroom is God as represented in Jesus Christ. *Song of Solomon* is filled with a myriad of symbolism.

Unless examined individually, the symbols can be as confusing as the symbolism in *Revelation.*

Dr. Bhatti has gone deep into the meaning of every symbol. He explores it with his own Christology of love. Coming from the Muslim lands of Pakistan with where Allah is seen as capricious and judgmental, Dr. Bhatti instead finds the missing theological ingredient: God's incredible love for his creation.

In *A Duet of Christ and Church,* Dr. Bhatti does not produce a dry reading. Instead, the reader is swept along in an incredible journey. Yes, it is a love story, the ultimate of love stories.

Dr. Bhatti has done what few other theologians have dared to do. He comes to terms with one of the most difficult books of the Bible, shedding a new light on the *Song of Solomon.* He has blown away the dust of the ages, showing us why the ancient Hebrews felt this book belongs in the Hebrew canon.

I trust you will find it as fascinating and insightful as I did when I held the manuscript in my hands. Read it slowly as he covers so much in each of its amazing pages. Having known Dr. Bhatti for many years, his scholarship does not disappoint the reader. He has always been brave to tackle the most difficult, bringing to life new discoveries while no doubt revealing those facts long forgotten by time.

I have no doubt that *A Duet of Christ and Church* will set a new standard of study and appreciation for the long overlooked *Song of Solomon.*

--Most Rev. Dr. Jan L. Beaderstadt
Archbishop, Worldwide Anglican Church

1

1:1

The Song of songs, which is Solomon's.

Solomon was the wisest man on this earth. God's wisdom was in his heart. People from different nations were eager to hear the wisdom he had. His wisdom was greater than all the people in different nations around him. If the wisdom he had was his own wisdom, he would not have been so respected among the nations. The nations around him saw a level of wisdom which was not found in any of the other residents (in any other nation) on the surface of the earth.

1-Kings 4:32-33

He spoke three thousand proverbs; and his songs numbered one thousand five. He spoke of trees, from the cedar that is in Lebanon even to the hyssop that grows out of the wall; he also spoke of animals, of birds, of creeping things, and of fish.

Some people think that the Song of Songs is not written by Solomon. They think that the people near the borders of Israel used to sing these songs at their weddings so this book could not be the work of Solomon. Some people doubt that this book is a revelation of God. The reason they don't accept that Song of Songs is a divine book is because it is written by Solomon, who fell from the right path because of his many wives. People think that Solomon wrote it in the love of one of his wives. So the question arises as to how this book can be a divine revelation?

To clear this doubt, let's compare Solomon to one of the most respected prophets in the Old Testament. Some people think that Moses was the most respected prophet among all the prophets of the Old Testament. According to them, Solomon wasn't even close to Moses in any way. But when we examine them both, we see many qualities which Moses had, Solomon had as well. People respect King David because God said, "he is according to my heart" but they often forget the fact that God preferred Solomon over David to build the temple. If David loved God, Solomon also loved God (1-Kings 3:3-5). Certainly, God saw something good in Solomon and He selected Solomon out of all the sons David had. God didn't only select Solomon out of all the house of David, but out of the whole world. He selected a single person to build the temple and that was Solomon. 1-Kings 10:9 say, *"Blessed is Yahweh your God, who delighted in you, to set you on the throne of Israel. Because Yahweh loved Israel forever, therefore he made you king, to do justice and righteousness"*. God appointed Solomon as king over Israel because he loved Israel. Solomon was a gift of God to Israel. He never gives a wrong or bad gift to His children (Matthew 7:9-11), so at that time, Solomon was the best person to be ruler over Israel.

Moses is a highly respected prophet, because, through him, God gave the Law and the pattern of the Tabernacle. When we compare Moses and Solomon, we see that the laws regarding rituals were given to Moses but the laws regarding wisdom were given by God through Solomon, in the book of Proverbs. Moses prepared the worship place (tabernacle) according to the pattern given by God (Exodus 25:9); Solomon also built the worship place (temple) under the guidance of God (1-Chronicles 28:11-12). Moses encouraged people and they bought gifts to build the tabernacle (Exodus 35:21-24). In the time of David and Solomon, people brought gifts to build the temple (1-Chronicles 29:1-10). God appeared to Moses

(Exodus 3:1-5); He also appeared to Solomon (1-Kings 9:2). When Moses finished the work, God's cloud and anointing rested upon the tabernacle (Exodus 40:34-35, Leviticus 9:22-24). When Solomon finished the temple, God consecrated the temple in the same way that He consecrated the tabernacle (2-Chronicles 5:13-14, 7:1). In this way, we see that Solomon wasn't less than Moses and David in his spiritual experiences. So we shouldn't look down on Solomon assuming that he can't have a revelation from God in the form of Song of Songs.

If Solomon's services to God were almost the same as Moses', then why we should look down at Solomon? Although we see that Solomon fell from God's standards by worshiping idols most of the Bible teachers believe that he repented before his death. It is human nature that we remember bad things more than the good acts of a man. It is believed that the book of Ecclesiastes is proof of his repentance, as most of the Bible scholars believe that it was written in his old age. Whereas this book, Song of Songs, was written in his youth before he fell into sin. It testified for him that he loved God (1-Kings3:3-5). Therefore the Song of Songs can't be a worldly book. The books of Proverbs and Ecclesiastes are the excellent work of Solomon. If God can give two holy books by Solomon, why should we doubt that He can't give the third book through him? Song of Songs is an excellent book to understand the relation between a husband and wife and also between Jesus and the Church as bridegroom and bride. The phrase, "Song of Songs" means "the best song" written by Solomon. If the wisest man on earth says that this is the best of his work, then we should take it seriously because it was not his wisdom by which he described things but God's wisdom.

1:2

Let him kiss me with the kisses of his mouth; for your love is better than wine.

This is the expression of the love of the lady for her beloved. It's necessary to express our love for our spouse in real life because it is written that, *"Better is open rebuke than hidden love"* (Proverbs 27:5). When we express our love, it gives strength to our relationship. It is also necessary to express our love for God. When we worship, we express our love for Him and when we obey His commands we give proof of our love. If we love Him, we will obey Him. The lady in this verse wants her beloved to kiss her. She is not asking for one or two kisses, she is asking for many kisses; she wants a continual expression of love from her beloved. A kiss in the Bible represents love and respect (Proverbs 24:26). When Judas the Iscariot came to Jesus, he kissed Him to show his respect (deceitfully). It was their custom to show respect by kissing. For others there, this kiss was a sign to attack. The kisses of unfaithful people hurt Jesus' feelings and the real church.

The bride wants her bridegroom to show His love. She wants intimate love which may last for a long time because she is asking for many kisses. This is the love church should have for Jesus. She wants to continually stay in touch with Christ. Christians shouldn't stay from Jesus even for a short while. The love of Christ is more delightful than wine. The people who love wine don't want to live without it. Whether they have something to eat or not, they prefer wine more than anything else. The bride is so deep in the love of the groom that her love is deeper than any other thing in this world. The kisses of the bridegroom show the love for His bride and the words of the bride show her love for the bridegroom, which is Jesus Christ our Lord and savior.

1:3

Your oils have a pleasing fragrance. Your name is oil poured out, therefore the virgins love you.

The bride is praising the fragrance of the perfumes used by the bridegroom. Normally in the Bible, a fragrance used by humans in the presence of God represents worship but the fragrance of perfumes of the bridegroom here represents different kinds of anointing, describing aspects of Jesus (Isaiah 11:1-3). Each fragrance shows a different anointing and ministry of Jesus. The works we see in His life, like teaching, healing, deliverance, etc represent different kinds of anointing. At one place He is teaching, other places He is healing, and then on some other place, He is showing miracles. Every aspect of His life is wonderful. The fragrance of a man comes when a man is physically present somewhere. So the fragrance of Christ also represents His presence somewhere. In Mark 16:20, "*They went out, and preached everywhere, the Lord working with them, and confirming the word by the signs that followed. Amen.*" The signs and wonders which were taking place were tangible proof of Jesus' presence, power, and authority. In this way, Jesus' fragrance is spreading all over the world. This fragrance is still the same because Jesus' power never declines. He is the same today, yesterday, and forever. It is still the case that when His people, pray miracles do happen. His name is like perfume poured out because when we call upon His name, His presence comes and wonders started taking place.

Mark 16:17-18

These signs will accompany those who believe: in my name they will cast out demons; they will speak with new languages; they will take up serpents; and if they drink any deadly thing, it will in no way hurt them; they will lay hands on the sick, and they will recover.

Luke 10:17-19

The seventy returned with joy, saying, "Lord, even the demons are subject to us in your name!" He said to them, "I saw Satan having fallen like lightning from heaven. Behold, I give you authority to tread on serpents and scorpions, and over all the power of the enemy. Nothing will in any way hurt you. Nevertheless, don't rejoice in this, that the spirits are subject to you, but rejoice that your names are written in heaven."

In Mark 16:17-18, Jesus commanded his disciples to pray and perform miracles in His name. In Luke 10:19, we see the practical impact of the words of Jesus in the life of disciples. This impact is still as powerful as it was during the earthly life of Jesus. There isn't any human who can perform true miracles in his own name or in any other name than that of Jesus. When we call upon His name, His presence comes and glorifies His name by performing the miracle we need. In this way, His name carries the very fragrance (presence) of Jesus.

The man's fragrance is experienced only by the people who come near him. The young women are crazy about His fragrance. At many points in the Bible, women represent nations. God's salvation plan is not only for one nation or tribe. It is for nations. He is the God of nations. His house is the house of prayer for all the nations. Today the solution for the problems of the world is only one name, and that is Jesus. Jesus sent His disciples to all the nations, not to a single nation. His name, His fragrance, is wonderful and that's why women (nations) are longing for Him.

1:4

Take me away with you. Let's hurry. The king has brought me into his rooms. We will be glad and rejoice in you. We will praise your love more than wine! They are right to love you.

The bride wants to go with the bridegroom. She doesn't want to be in this world. This is the cry of the church even in these days. When we see all the corruption in the world, the way the world mocks Christians, how they want to drive the world according to Satan, then the bride (church) pleads to Christ to come and take her away with Him (2-Corinthians 5:2-4). Every true believer desires to stay in the chamber of the king (Jesus). When we study the lives of Moses, Joshua, Daniel, and David, they always wanted to be in His presence (Psalms 27:4). The king brought the bride to His chamber. No one can go to King's chamber until invited by the king. Jesus has invited people from all nations to be His bride. We see this crowd in the book of Revelation.

Revelation 7:9-10

After these things I looked, and behold, a great multitude, which no man could count, out of every nation and of all tribes, peoples, and languages, standing before the throne and before the Lamb, dressed in white robes, with palm branches in their hands. They cried with a loud voice, saying, "Salvation be to our God, who sits on the throne, and to the Lamb!"

They are the people who are counted as the bride of Christ. There is no limitation of color or race. Some people think that the Israelites are the only chosen people of God, but everyone who comes to Christ becomes a child of Abraham. Because Abraham is the father of believers and when Abraham becomes our father, we are counted as Israelites (spiritually).

In the second half of the verse, we hear the voice of more than one person committing themselves to delight in the king. The ones who are committing themselves are the virgins who are dedicating themselves to Solomon. The virgins here are representing people (2-Corinthians 11:2) from different nations and Solomon represents Jesus. The love of Christ has the same effect in the hearts of different people. They love Him more than wine, wealth, or any other thing. Wine controls the minds of people. When we come to Christ, everything which controls our mind has no more power over us. Anyone who prefers any other kind of wine over Christ, is not worthy of Christ. He loves us more than any other thing in the world and demands the same kind of dedication from us.

1:5-6

I am dark, but lovely, you daughters of Jerusalem, like Kedar's tents, like Solomon's curtains. Don't stare at me because I am dark, because the sun has scorched me. My mother's sons were angry with me. They made me keeper of the vineyards. I haven't kept my own vineyard.

Solomon was king. His bride tells the daughters of Jerusalem about herself. Daughters of Jerusalem represent the people in the church. In the book of Revelation, Jerusalem represents the bride of Christ which is the church (Revelation 21:2). So daughters of Jerusalem represent the people who are in Christ. We are called by the king of kings; this great invitation shouldn't make us boastful or proud. It is always recommended that we should keep in our mind our low spiritual condition from where God picked us up (Ezekiel 16:6). In the same way, although the bride is beloved of the bridegroom, she still remembers her past and her original state. In Deuteronomy 26, God taught about tithes and prayer regarding the first fruits. Like He taught the Lord's Prayer. In that prayer, Israelites needed to say, *"My father was a Syrian ready to perish. He went down into Egypt, and lived there, few in number. There he became a great, mighty, and populous nation. The Egyptians mistreated us, afflicted us, and imposed hard labor on us. Then we cried to Yahweh, the God of our fathers. Yahweh heard our voice, and saw our affliction, our toil, and our oppression. Yahweh brought us out of Egypt with a mighty hand, with an outstretched arm, with great terror, with signs, and with wonders.* (Deuteronomy 26:5-8).

The words of this prayer reminded the Israelites of their humble state. The bride remembered her past, saying that it is not because of my beauty that the king has picked me; it is all because of His grace. Her beauty wasn't enough to cause the king to pick her as His wife. When we keep in mind that we have come to a high position from a very low one, it keeps us humble, and humility is a key to success in the kingdom of God. Although Moses was a great leader, he was also the humblest man on the face of the earth (Numbers 12:3). The bride said that she is black like the tents of Kedar. Kedar was the people living in ancient Saudi Arabia. They used to make the covering of their tents from the hairs of black colored goats. The black color of her skin shows the hardships she had been going through. The black color of her skin is because she had been working under the sun. It was not her own choice that she had to work in the scorching heat. It wasn't some stranger who forced her to labor in the vineyard, but her relatives. They were her brothers. They didn't allow her to take care of her vineyard. Every one of us is answerable to God about his own vineyard. The bride left the fellowship where she wasn't allowed to take care of her vineyard. We need to leave such fellowships which are a hindrance in God's work. Because at the end of our life when we will reach in His presence, we would be asked about the work which was given to us, at that time if we will say that I didn't care for my vineyard because I was busy in someone else's vineyard then this would be an unacceptable answer.

The brothers of Joseph sold him to strangers and he worked there as a slave. Later, God delivered him from prison and made him a ruler in Egypt. In the same way, the brothers of the bride didn't deal well with her but the king picked her and brought her into His palace. The brothers used her for their profit. They had been sending her to take care of vineyards. In doing this, she was not able to establish her vineyard. This is a common tactic of Satan to keep us busy in other works. Sometimes he uses the people around us to keep us busy. We keep on thinking about providing for our family, kids, and other needs and keep on neglecting the call which Jesus has placed on our lives. When we come to Jesus, then He takes care of everything which belongs to us. In this way, he offers us a carefree life. In Matthew 8:21-22, Jesus had a conversation with a disciple;

Matthew 8:21-22

Another of his disciples said to him, "Lord, allow me first to go and bury my father." But Jesus said to him, "Follow me, and leave the dead to bury their own dead."

The man called himself a disciple of Christ; even then He was giving preference to other things over Jesus. Jesus is certainly not against taking care of parents. The disciple wanted to take care of his household until he became free from his responsibilities. A man never becomes free from his responsibilities throughout his life. It means that disciples would have never become available for ministry and Jesus wanted to save him from such circumstances. In the same way, the bride's brothers kept her busy in a business that took away all her beauty. But Solomon saved her from that brutal labor. Similarly, Jesus saves us from all kinds of labor of sin and brings us into His kingdom.

1:7-8

Tell me, you whom my soul loves, where you graze your flock, where you rest them at noon; for why should I be as one who is veiled beside the flocks of your companions? If you don't know,

most beautiful among women, follow the tracks of the sheep. Graze your young goats beside the shepherds' tents.

Tell me, you whom I love; the bride is asking a question to the bridegroom. The bride was in trouble, in her distress she called upon the bridegroom. There are times in our lives when we feel distressed as well. The question is, to whom we will call? When Saul had a problem, he went to a magician. Many times, when David had a problem, he humbled himself before God and God took him out of his troubles. Who we first turn to in our problems shows in whom we have our trust. Being the bride of Christ, we need to turn our face to Christ. The bride wanted to know about two places. One is the place where He grazes his flock and the second is the place where He rests at midday. The place where the flock grazes is the workplace of Solomon (Jesus). The place where He works is the place where His sheep get fed. If we see a church where there is no spiritual growth in the believers, it means the sheep there are not getting proper spiritual food. This shows that Christ is not working in that field or church. Being a worker in Lord's field, we should know the place where He wants us to work. We shouldn't choose our workplace on our own. We need to spend quality time at His feet to know the exact place where He wants us to work. God chose Peter to work among Jews and Paul to work among Gentiles. God wanted Jonah to work in Nineveh but he wanted to go to Tarsus. If you are hired by someone to work in a field then you can't go and work according to your wish. You have to fulfill the will of your owner. If we consider God as our Lord and owner then we need to please Him by working according to His plans. Jonah was running from God but you can't run from God. You may end up in a fish's belly. That would be a dead-end and you would have nowhere to go. From a dead-end, the only way is the way back. If we are running from God, every road will be a dead-end road. We need to go back and start all over again like the prodigal son.

For every person, God has a different plan. We need to know

that plan and place. Sometimes we keep on working in the wrong place, but when Jesus specified the exact place then Peter filled his boat with plenty of big fish. We need to know the right place, that's why the bride was asking her beloved the place where he works and the place where he rests. In verse 6 of the same chapter, she is saying that she is burnt by the sun because her brothers forced her to work in the sun. But, now she is under the protection of the bridegroom who takes care of His flock and keeps them under shade when the sun is burning hot. Jesus is the good shepherd who gives His own life for His flock. He calls all the heavy-laden to Him because He is the only one who can give them rest. His bride should follow Him but she didn't know where to go. It is the loyalty of the bride that she doesn't want to follow any other shepherd. She knows that if she should follow any other, it will be counted as adultery. When people leave their true God and follow other gods, it is known as spiritual adultery. God hates spiritual adultery which was the main reason that Israel went into slavery. They were following other gods. This is why the bride is saying, "why should I be as one who is veiled"? In ancient times a veil was used by prostitutes. Jesus' bride shouldn't be a veiled woman, like one says that "I belong to God" but in her heart, is following the pleasures of the world. The advice given, to find the shepherd, is to follow the tracks of the flock. This is the great advice we need to follow in our times as well. There are times in our lives when we are confused that which way we should go. In such a time we need to follow the pathways of the church which are given in the Bible. The whole Bible is a track record of His people; we can get the required guidance from that record.

1:9-11

I have compared you, my love, to a steed in Pharaoh's chariots. Your cheeks are beautiful with earrings, your neck with strings of jewels. We will make you earrings of gold, with studs of silver.

In verse 9, Solomon compared his beloved with a mare of Pharaoh's chariots. Chariots were used by kings and the officers of kings. Chariots and horses were efficient weapons of war against the enemy (Exodus 14:6-7, Proverbs 21:31). Chariots were also used for important announcements; Joseph was announced as second in command in Pharaoh's chariot (Genesis 41:43). They were a sign of someone's glory and riches. Joseph sent carts and animals for his father and brothers to carry them to Egypt. But, the chariot was only used by him (Genesis 46:29). When Jacob came to Egypt, Joseph came to meet him on his chariot, which shows Joseph's authority, respect, and riches in Egypt. Solomon called his beloved as a mare of Pharaoh's chariot because he had a very good knowledge of chariots and horses. Solomon had fourteen hundred chariots and twelve thousand horsemen in his army (1-Kings 10:26-28). Solomon was a major supplier of horses and chariots to the kings around him. It was one of his many businesses in which he was engaged.

2-Chronicles 1:16-17

The horses which Solomon had were brought out of Egypt and from Kue. The king's merchants purchased them from Kue. They brought up and brought out of Egypt a chariot for six hundred pieces of silver, and a horse for one hundred fifty. They also exported them to the Hittite kings and the Syrian kings.

When Joseph was the chief officer in Egypt, he was selling grain to the countries around him. When people didn't have any more money, they started selling their livestock (Genesis 47:15-18). These were very hard days in which only the strongest animals could survive. So when Joseph bought the animals, they were the best of best. In this way, Egypt became the most wealthy and powerful nation on the face of the earth. Livestock was counted as wealth, and so Egypt absorbed the wealth of the countries around it. Egypt didn't only have the wealth of people around it, by buying horses from other countries; Egypt shattered the military power of other countries. It means Egypt had the best horses in the time of Joseph. In this way when Solomon compared his beloved with one of the mares of Pharaoh's chariots, it means he was comparing her with one of the best of best in the world. The horses which were usually used in a king's chariot were very powerful and highly trained horses, trained to obey their master instantly. Solomon sees his beloved as a mare that is powerful, obedient, and ready to do anything on the command of her master. The characteristics of such horses are further explained by God in the book of Job; if we look at these characteristics spiritually, we can learn many reasons why Jesus compared His bride with a mare.

Job 39:19-25,

"Have you given the horse might? Have you clothed his neck with a quivering mane? Have you made him to leap as a locust? The glory of his snorting is awesome. He paws in the valley, and rejoices in his strength. He goes out to meet the armed men. He mocks at fear, and is not dismayed, neither does he turn back from the sword. The quiver rattles against him, the flashing spear and the javelin. He eats up the ground with fierceness and rage, neither does he stand still at the sound of the trumpet. As often as the trumpet sounds he snorts, 'Aha!' He smells the battle afar off, the thunder of the captains, and the shouting.

God desires that His people become swift in obeying His commands. This is why when Jesus taught the prayer to His disciples; He asked them to pray, *"Let your Kingdom come. Let your will be done on earth as it is in heaven"* (Matthew 6:10). Jesus wants His people to fulfill His will as His will is fulfilled in heaven. Whereas in heaven,

His will is fulfilled without any delays. In heaven, His angels fulfill His will without wasting any time. He wants His people to respond in the same way.

The bridegroom is praising the cheeks of His beloved. When people meet each other, they look at the face of each other. The very first impression of beauty appears with someone's face, and cheeks are the main part of anyone's face. The face shows the evidence of likes or dislikes. So by looking at the face or cheeks of the bride, Solomon saw acceptance for himself. It is a big question for us today whether Jesus feels welcomed when He looks at us, or do we just go to church because we want to please our pastor or parents? Cheeks don't only show our expressions to others, cheeks are also where others show their expressions by kissing them. In almost all the cultures parents and relatives show their love by kissing on the cheeks of children. In some cultures when people meet each other, they show their respect by kissing each other on the cheeks. Cheeks are sometimes like a health certificate of a person. By looking at someone's face we can say that the person is weak or normal. By praising the cheeks, the bridegroom is saying that the first impression the bride shows is amazing. Similarly, whenever Jesus looks at His bride, He feels love and compassion for the church.

In the same verse, the bridegroom is talking about the neck of His beloved. Medically, the neck is a very important part of our body. Both front and back of the neck carry important structures for our life. The front part is necessary for taking a breath whereas, the back of the neck carries neurons to send signals to the brain. So our neck is the main hub through which signals passes and the brain becomes able to control the whole body. The neck is the body part from where we can produce sounds to express our needs or emotions.

The bridegroom is also talking about the pearl necklaces on the neck of the bride. Normally pearls are white color but other colors are also available. Pearls are made by an oyster that is found in the sea. When a sand grain or food particle enters an oyster, the oyster feels irritation, and to get rid of that irritation, the oyster starts covering it with some chemical. When this covering keeps on growing, a time comes when the process is complete and that thing takes the form of a pearl. This is not an easy or quick process. Sometimes it takes months and sometimes it takes years to complete.

Our lives are like the lives of an oyster. When we listen or read the Word of God, it goes inside us like a small grain of sand or spiritual food. That grain or seed of the Word starts challenging our souls. We ask God to give us an understanding of the Word. Now we start meditating about the Word. As the oyster covers the sand grain with chemical (nacre), meditation is like a spiritual chemical which changes a specific verse into a revelation. This revelation sparkles like a costly pearl in our lives. The more we read the Bible, the more verses become the part of our soul, the more we meditate on different verses, the more pearls we will have. The more pearls we have, the more necklaces we will have around our necks. Jesus is not talking about a single necklace. He is talking about more than one necklace. When we meditate about different topics, each Biblical topic has several verses. When we meditate about those verses, they form different necklaces around our necks. Jesus didn't tell us how many necklaces there are on the neck. It depends on how much we meditate about Jesus and His word, as to how our necklaces will keep on growing. One thing we need to keep in mind is that we can't produce the revelations on our own. Jesus is the one who reveals His word. His Holy Spirit changes the words into revelations. So revelations, which are like spiritual pearls for us, are not the result of our own efforts. These are the gifts of the Holy Spirit which lead us to spiritual growth. When Jesus looks at us, the necklaces/ revelations make the bride attractive. When these revelations surround our neck, they will guard the words which will come out of our mouth. Then the words of our speech and imaginations of our hearts will be acceptable to God (Psalm 19:14).

In verse 10 of the first chapter of Song of Songs, the bridegroom talks about the necklaces of pearls. In verse 11, he talks about other ornaments that will be given by the groom to the bride. These ornaments would be made of gold with some work of silver in them. Gold and silver were widely used in making different instruments in the tabernacle of Moses, in the Old Testament. In that formation, gold represents divinity and silver represents salvation. But you will not see even a single instrument in which gold and silver both are used. The ornament the groom promised to the bride is the one in which the base is gold and then silver is studded in it. It means God will provide salvation. Salvation can't come from any other side in the life of a believer. We can't earn salvation; it is a gift of God that is promised by the Messiah to His beloved church. This gift is given after the gift of necklaces in verse 10. We have already seen that necklaces represent revelations and the ornament in verse 11 represents the work of salvation. There are three types of salvation. The first type of salvation is that which we get when we repent from our sins like the thief on the cross. The second kind of salvation is that which we get step by step in our Christian life. When we first repent from our sins, our spirit is saved but some bad habits are not gone immediately, like anger, lies, and other unseemly habits. These habits leave our lives when we keep on walking with Christ. The disciples accepted Christ when Jesus called them, but throughout His earthly life He kept on correcting them. In the same way, different churches in the book of Revelation got salvation after repentance but Jesus pointed out the mistakes in their lives. The third kind of salvation is the salvation which we will get when we go to heaven. While we are in this body there will be different tests and trials which we have to endure. But, in heaven, we will be free from all kinds of sickness, disease, worries, disappointments, and tests.

We start getting revelations from God after our repentance. If pearls are revelations and revelations are received after salvation, then it means the salvation (gold ornaments with silver workmanship in verse 11) is the second type of salvation which is ongoing salvation in our earthly life.

1: 12-14

While the king sat at his table, my perfume spread its fragrance. My beloved is to me a sachet of myrrh, that lies between my breasts. My beloved is to me a cluster of henna blossoms from the vineyards of En Gedi.

Normally the king doesn't eat alone. Several people eat along with him. 2-Samuel 9:10-11, 1-Samual 20:23-27, 1-Kings 2:7, 10:5, and Nehemiah 5:17 shows that kings sit with the high-ranking officers and guests when they eat. In Matthew 26:6-7 a woman came and anointed His head with perfume while He was at the table with His disciples and other guests who were invited by the house owner named Simon. So this scenario was the same as the king who is taking the meal at the table and other people are around him. While He was eating a woman broke the perfume bottle and put the very expensive perfume on His head. Having a nice soothing smell while eating a meal was hardly available to a common man, provision of that kind of aroma was very difficult. Perfumes were considered as priced treasures of kings. When the king of Babylon came to visit Hezekiah, Hezekiah showed him all his treasures which included precious perfumes as well (Isaiah 39:1-2). The provision of the perfumed atmosphere during the meal was a delicacy for very special events. We are the treasured possession of our God. We are the bride of Christ. We need to show our love and reverence to Christ in worship. Our worship is the precious perfume we provide in His presence. When we provide these things to others, He doesn't like it.

Ezekiel 23:40-41

"Furthermore you sisters have sent for men who come from far away, to whom a messenger was sent, and behold, they came; for whom you washed yourself, painted your eyes, decorated yourself with ornaments,

and sat on a stately bed, with a table prepared before it, whereupon you set my incense and my oil.

According to Proverbs 27:9, *"Perfume and incense bring joy to the heart".* As our worship works as a perfume; which brings joy to Christ. It is not necessary that we only worship Him when we spend time in church or our prayer. When our thought life is focused on Him and we keep on thinking about our beloved Jesus then this is the sweet aroma that is valued by Christ.

In verse 13, the bride is expressing her love by saying that *"My beloved is to me a sachet of myrrh, that lies between my breasts".* The night is the time when we take a rest. She says that even at night time I have Him with me in my thoughts. When we put on some perfume, it creates an environment around us. Whoever comes near us, will feel that environment of the sweet smell. The bride is saying that my beloved is like a sweet smell with me. It means I am wrapped in the environment of my beloved Jesus. The environment is created by a specific kind of smell which is "myrrh". Myrrh was used frequently in the temple, and it produces a sweet smell by burning it. A sweet-smelling smoke comes out of the censers of the priest. The atmosphere of myrrh, in which the priest spent time during the day, remained to feed him at night. We are the kingly priests of the present days (1-Peter 2:9). The environment in which we will live during the day will be with us at night as well. If we spend our time doing wrong things in the day, the same kind of thoughts will surround us at night. When we get up in the morning, we will find ourselves influenced to act according to the thoughts which were with us last night. The people, who live a life of worship, keep on worshiping the Lord through their words and acts throughout the day. The ultimate result of worship is anointing because anointing comes by worship. During the day they spend time with Christ, and at night He spends time with them by wrapping them in His anointing. Whenever Jesus taught to people or disciples, always there was anointing with Him. In the Old Testament, when He gave His teachings in the form of the Law of Moses, there was an anointing.

In Job 33:14-15, it is written, "*For God speaks once, yes twice, though man pays no attention. In a dream, in a vision of the night, when deep sleep falls on men, in slumbering on the bed*". The anointing of God remains with His people even at night time and He teaches them, reveals secrets to them, and tells them the future. He had been teaching Joseph (son of Jacob), Daniel, Joseph (father of Jesus), and many other people at night in the dreams. So His presence remains with His people day and night. Our worship is like a sweet smell to Him and His presence is a sweet smell to us. This is the sachet of myrrh, the feel of His presence, the bride is talking about.

To describe her love and closeness with the groom, the bride describes the bridegroom as a sachet of myrrh which lies in between her breasts. Regarding breasts, different Bible teachers give different views but I like the view that two breasts are two covenants that is Old Testament and New Testament. For a child, the breast is a blessing because it feeds the child, and for a husband, the breast satisfies his desires as well. Spiritually we need the milk of the Word of God to grow. This spiritual feed we get from the Old and New Testaments. The bride says that the bridegroom is in between the breasts. If two breasts are two covenants then Jesus is the mediator of two covenants, the person who is in between two covenants. The new covenant didn't start with the birth of Christ but with the death of Jesus Christ (Hebrews 8:6, 9:15, 12:24). So the time he spent in his earthly body (approximately thirty three years) was the time between two covenants. In this way, Jesus became the mediator of two covenants which was portrayed by Solomon hundreds of years before the birth of Christ.

The personality of Jesus has different aspects. In this verse, another aspect of Christ's personality is discussed by comparing Him with the cluster of henna from EinGedi. So we will discuss EinGedi and henna in this section. EinGedi means "spring of Kid (young goat)". It is located to the west of the Dead Sea. It was in the territory of Judah (Joshua 15:62). In this area, David had been hiding when he was running from Saul (1-Samuel 23:29, 24:1). Ezekiel talked prophetically about this place (Ezekiel 47:10). EinGedi on the whole is a dry place but a small area of this place has sprung and shows a whole different view of this place. This small area is a nature reserve in Israel. Henna and many other flowering plants are found here. Archaeologists have found proof that henna was being used in the Middle Bronze Age, which is about 1900 to 1500 BCE, in the land of Israel or Canaan. Henna is known for its' color and sweet smell all over the world. Flowers of henna from EinGedi were being used for decoration and perfumes. Sometimes people keep the leaves and flowers of henna in their houses, so the good smell will fill their home.

Henna represents Christ's love for His bride. Henna leaves are first crushed, made into a paste and then they are applied on hands, feet, or hair. When the paste dries up, it is washed and it leaves a beautiful red color on the skin or hair, where it was applied. Christ was crushed by the stripes on His back. By crushing the henna leaves, its color comes out and by crushing Jesus, his blood came out. Like henna, the blood of Christ is applied to different organs of our body and it gives a soothing effect by healing them. The color we get from His affliction can be seen in the form of our salvation. The sweet smell of the Christ our Lord is spreading around through His people. People can see and realize the presence of Jesus through our acts. As the smell of henna and the color of henna can't be hidden, so no matter whatever the enemy will do, His people can't remain hidden. They will keep on spreading the good news of salvation (2-Corinthians 2:15).

1:15

Behold, you are beautiful, my love. Behold, you are beautiful. Your eyes are like doves.

The bridegroom praises His bride. He praises her in two ways. First, He praises her for what she is, and secondly, He praises her for what she is for Him. First He says that you are beautiful then He says that you are my darling, you are my beloved. But a question arises, was the bride beautiful in other people's eyes as well? In my opinion, she was not beautiful to other people, because in Song of Songs 1:6, she admits that there is no beauty of her own in her. She said that she is black, burnt by the sun. In ancient times, people mistreated blacks, they used them as slaves. But, Jesus, without thinking about the color or creed, welcomes everyone into His church. The woman looked black, which was not a mark of beauty for others but for Jesus, our bridegroom, she is precious than anything in the universe. By looking at God's dealing with Israel/ bride, some people think that God has favoritism in His dealing with humans. But, this thinking is limited by their narrow vision. All people are God's creation. He sent His Son for everyone and shed His blood equally for everyone. So there is no racism in Christ. He came for everyone who is lost. He sent Philip to the black Ethiopian, He sent Peter to gentiles and Paul to different nations because He loves all the souls.

The bridegroom is not impressed by the outward look of the bride, but He is talking about her inner beauty. The inner beauty of the bride could be seen by her eyes. Her eyes are like a dove. The dove is considered as a bird that represents purity and peace. The dove was also used in the ritual cleansing of the sinners in the temple. If a poor man commits some sin and he didn't have enough resources to bring a goat or lamb, then he was allowed to bring a dove (Leviticus 5:7). So, when the bridegroom says that you have dove eyes it means His bride has purity in her eyes. Our eyes and ears are doors to our minds. When our eyes are pure, it means our thoughts are pure. So being the bride of Christ, church people must have purity in their eyes which leads to pure thoughts.

1:16

Behold, you are beautiful, my beloved, yes, pleasant; and our couch is verdant.

The bride is praising her groom. For the bride, her groom is handsome and charming. Many verses in the Bible talk about the appearance of Christ. To Abraham, He appeared as Melchizedek, king of Salem (Genesis 14:18). To Jacob, He appeared as a wrestler (Genesis 32:24). To Moses, he appeared as "I am who I am" (Exodus 3:14). He appeared to seventy elders of Israel (Exodus 24:10). He appeared to Joshua as the captain of the Lord's armies. He appeared to Ezekiel as a man on the throne of an awesome crystal (Ezekiel 1:4-28). In some translations the name of this crystal is lapis lazuli. To John, He appeared as the one who has the keys of death and Hades (Revelation 1:12-18).To different people, he gave different revelations of His personality. In Matthew 16:13-19, Jesus asked two questions to His disciples. The first question was, "Who do men say that I, the Son of Man, am?" and the second question was, "who do you say that I am?"

Matthew 16:13-19

Now when Jesus came into the parts of Caesarea Philippi, he asked his disciples, saying, "Who do men say that I, the Son of Man, am?" They said, "Some say John the Baptizer, some, Elijah, and others, Jeremiah or one of the prophets." He said to them, "But who do you say that I am?" Simon Peter answered, "You are the Christ, the Son of the living God." Jesus answered him, "Blessed are you, Simon Bar Jonah, for flesh and blood has not revealed this to you, but my Father who is in heaven. I also tell you that you are Peter, and on this rock I will build my assembly, and the gates of Hades will not prevail against it. I will give to you the keys of the Kingdom of Heaven, and whatever you bind on earth will have been bound in heaven; and whatever you release on earth will have been released in heaven."

Jesus has the same two questions for the present-day church as well. The answer to the first question, *"Who do men say that I, the Son of Man, am?"* shows what we know about Jesus from other sources. These sources may include our parents, some Christian books, our pastor, or any other source from where we come to know about Christ. These sources are important but our Christian life cannot be built on the basis of the knowledge we get from others. We should have a personal relationship with Christ. The second question of Jesus, *"who do you say that I am?"* Points out our relationship with Jesus. The beauty of Christian life doesn't flourish if we don't have intimacy with Jesus.

The bride adores the beauty of the groom which shows the closeness bride has with the groom. It is not by the personal efforts of the bride that she can know the beauty of the bridegroom. It is only possible by the grace of the bridegroom. Jesus praised Peter because to Peter, the Holy Spirit revealed a secret about Jesus. When the Holy Spirit gave revelation to Peter, Jesus said that He will build His church on that revelation, and the gates of hell would not be able to overcome that church. Revelations reveal Jesus to us and only then we become able to say to Jesus that, "you are beautiful".

In this verse, the bride talks about the color of the bed, which is verdant/ green. The green color represents fertility and growth. The bed is the place where the bride and bridegroom show their love to each other. It is a place of intimacy. The color of that place (bed) is green, which means the intimacy between the bride and bridegroom is growing. Intimacy is the basic requirement of a relationship to grow. A lack of intimacy leads to failure in relationships. The intimacy of the church should grow over time. If it is not growing, then we will remain immature Christians (Hebrews 5:12).

1:17

The beams of our house are cedars. Our rafters are firs.

Rafters and beams are important parts of the structure of a roof. Without them, you can't complete a house. The bride is saying that the beams are made of cedars and rafters are made of firs (in some translations cypress). Cedar and fir trees are mentioned several times in the Bible. In some cultures the cedar tree is known as the tree of life because it has a long life span, it is strong, tall, and has many medicinal benefits. The fir is also well known for its quality to build houses and medicinal qualities. Cedar and fir both are quite expensive woods. Both grow to a good height and give shadow, but a fir's shadow is denser than the cedar.

In the Israelite culture, a bride leaves the house of her father and goes to the groom's house (Genesis 24:53-67, 1- Samuel 25:39-42). It is the responsibility of the bridegroom to prepare a place for the bride. Our bridegroom (Jesus) is well aware of His responsibilities. Therefore He has already gone to prepare a place for us (John 14:2-3). We can have a glimpse of the place in Revelation 21. As the bride is giving reference to the expensive woods used in making the house, it shows the value bridegroom is giving to the bride that He is willing to provide the best for His beloved. Cedar and cypress/ fir wood was used in the Temple of Solomon (1-Kings 5:6-8, 6:15-16, 6:34). Cedar represents saints (Psalms 92:12, 104:16), and musical instruments were made from fir wood. *David and all the house of Israel played before Yahweh with all kinds of instruments made of cypress wood, with harps, with stringed instruments, with tambourines, with castanets, and with cymbals* (2-Samuel 6:5). It means the two trees represent saints and their worship. In the heavenly house of the bride, the saints will be there and they will be worshiping the Lamb.

2

2:1

I am a rose of Sharon, a lily of the valleys.

The bride introduces herself and she says that she is a rose and a lily. The Rose of Sharon is not a rose we normally have in our minds. It is a delicate flower that comes in different colors with a long stamen. It is a relatively hardy shrub, tolerant to different kinds of soils. It is also known as Hibiscus. Some people think that the Rose of Sharon is a leafy plant which can survive for many days even in hard weather conditions. The Lily of the Valley is a white-colored bell-shaped flower with a sweet scent. It is famous for its perfume and is often made in cologne. It is used to cure many illnesses like heart disease, epilepsy, kidney problems, etc. It is poisonous for animals if ingested.

By looking at the facts about the rose of Sharon and lily of the valley, we see that the church is a plant like the rose of Sharon which can withstand different weather conditions. It can survive, without complaining, in hard times when there is a shortage of supplies. History has proved this fact over and over again. In the early days of Christianity, Roman emperors and soldiers tried to subdue Christians. It was a time like hard weather. The persecution of Christians started in 64 AD and continued until 313 AD. In this whole time, Christians did not attack the state, *but were persecuted by the state.* The more it tried to eliminate Christianity, using its great resources, the more Christianity grew. Romans thought that Christians were not loyal to the Roman Empire. Christians had been talking about the kingdom of God, and Jesus as the king. Romans wanted Christians to worship the Roman king and not think about any other king. When Christians refused to worship Roman Kings, it was considered as rebellion against the king and kingdom. So Christians were ordered to be killed. In history, the kings who wanted to see the fear of death on the faces of Christians never had their desire fulfilled. Christians were often happy when they faced the sword or when they were thrown in front of wild animals to be torn apart; there was a smile on their faces. This smile angered the Romans. Christians happily accepted the persecution because life or death couldn't separate them from their beloved Christ. Death opens a door through which we can enter and stay with Jesus forever. Therefore Christians didn't take into account the pains in this world; they considered the joy which was lying ahead of them.

The bride compares herself with lily of valley. The lily is a poisonous plant but it is used for many medicinal purposes. The flowers look beautiful and white in color, but nobody should be deceived by its beauty and tenderness into believing they can eliminate its presence from the earth. Lily represents the church; nobody should think that the church looks like a harmless beautiful flower, so they can eliminate the church from this earth. The Romans tried to do it. They lost their own kingdom and presence but the church didn't leave its place; it kept on flourishing. Paul tried to stop Christianity from flourishing but he eventually joined the church. Hitler wanted to erase God's people but he was erased from this earth. Those in history, who tried to stand against His bride, the church, found that the bride did nothing to retaliate but the bridegroom protected her. In the beginning, opponents felt that they were succeeding, and the church often looks like it is defeated, but history shows that to be untrue. When oppression came, the early church did not respond with violence toward her oppressors. Opponents always try to subdue the church with power, money, and bloodshed. The church remains quiet; in her quietness is her strength. The church always asks Jesus to step in, When He steps in, He asks every Paul about why He is persecuting His bride?

2:2

As a lily among thorns, so is my love among the daughters.

The bridegroom loves the bride so much that all other women in comparison to her look like thorns and the bride looks like a flower. A flower gives beauty; it is a soft and beautiful entity in nature. Thorns, on the other hand, are hard and often harm the people who touch them but a flower gives a soft touch to everyone and unforgettable fragrance. Women in the Bible often represent different nations. So basically, Jesus is comparing His bride/ Christian nation with other nations.

When God looks at the church, for Him it is like a flower among the other nations of the world. God loves every nation, but in their behavior, they are like thorns. Throughout history, many nations tried to trample the flower of the church. The church remained silent. If you think about any other nation, they would pick up their weapons to fight in defense against another nation's attacks on them. In this way, they cut each other's throats and blood runs like water in the streets. In the present-day, you can see that Christians are persecuted for their faith in different parts of the world but they are not answering their oppressors with any kind of militant attack. If we look at some other nations, we will see several terrorist organizations that are working to protect their people. The church doesn't believe in shedding the blood of others. They believe that as Jesus shed His blood for others, we need to follow the same model to show the love of Christ. The church is being bled in different parts of the world. Church buildings are being bombed. Many Christians are murdered every year. Christian girls are kidnapped, raped, forcefully married into other religions, and sold in human markets, but nobody is taking notice. Although all kinds of thorns are around the church, the church is still giving its fragrance to the world. By looking at different NGOs and INGOs around the world, we see that most of them are funded by faith-based organizations; for example, Samaritan's Purse, Lutheran World Relief, etc. Jesus had been doing everything good for humanity but in the end, He was crucified. The process of crucifixion never stopped. First, it was Christ, who was crucified, now it is His body, the church which is being constantly persecuted on the cross. Jesus looks with favor on His bride and the bride says,*"Who shall separate us from the love of Christ? Could oppression, or anguish, or persecution, or famine, or nakedness, or peril, or sword? Even as it is written, "For your sake we are killed all day long. We were accounted as sheep for the slaughter." No, in all these things, we are more than conquerors through him who loved us. For I am persuaded that neither death, nor life, nor angels, nor principalities, nor things present, nor things to come, nor powers, nor height, nor depth, nor any other created thing will be able to separate us from God's love which is in Christ Jesus our Lord."* (Romans 8:35-39).

2:3

As the apple tree among the trees of the wood, so is my beloved among the sons. I sat down under his shadow with great delight, his fruit was sweet to my taste.

Most of the trees in the jungle have good shade but not good fruit. Apple tree height varies between 10 to 39 feet. So the apple trees have fruit and shade both. The bride compares the bridegroom to an apple tree. To her, the bridegroom is the only wonderful tree that has fruit, shade, and a sweet fragrance. Other trees (gods) either don't have fruit or their state is like the fig tree which had the appearance of a fruit-bearing tree but it didn't have any fruit. In Luke 13:6-9, Jesus compared people with fruitful and unfruitful trees. Fruit also represents the works of people (Matthew 3:8, 7:16).

Fruitful trees are people in God's orchard who are doing their best to obey God and do the works the Holy Spirit asks them to do. God is perfecting us on this earth before we go to heaven. He keeps on working on fruitful trees. He prunes them; which can be a painful process in life. In the process of pruning, gardeners cut off the branches which can hinder the productivity of plants. Cutting off the branches means removing such habits or relationships which are a hindrance to our spiritual prosperity. If someone is addicted to drugs and after coming to Christ, has to leave this habit, it won't be an easy task for them. Similarly, if a man used to take bribes in his office, then to grow in Christ, he has to leave this habit. This won't be an easy task for him because he was spending as much as he wanted; now he has to be confined to what his original salary is. Bearing fruit is not the only task in God's kingdom. An unfruitful tree should bear fruit and a fruitful tree needs to increase its yield. The good news in all this process is that, God is with us and His Word strengthens us (2-Corinthians 12:9). So we grow from strength to strength and our fruitfulness keeps on increasing till the end of our lives.

Christ is a fruitful tree who doesn't need any pruning because he always does whatever the Father asks Him to do (John 5:19). It is an honor to sit under His shade. When we are under His shade then He bears the heat of the day and we enjoy the shade. When Jacob went to meet his uncle and Rachel came to the well, Jacob removed the stone to quench the thirst of Rachel's goats; although it was against the rule of shepherds to give water to folks at that time (Genesis Chapter 29). As Jacob was standing for Rachel, so Rachel was under his shade. In the New Testament, Jesus saved a woman who was caught in the act of adultery; but as she was depending on Jesus for her safety, so she was sitting under His shade. A Greek woman came to Jesus. Her daughter was possessed by demons. To test her faith Jesus didn't pay any attention to her but kept on walking. She fell on His feet and worshiped Him. This was the sign that, although she was a Gentile, she accepted the supremacy of Jesus over all the idols she had been worshiping throughout her life. Indirectly she was requesting Him to let her take rest under His shade, something her idols weren't able to this for her. Jesus accepted her request. By coming under His shade, she left the shade of other gods she had been worshiping and Jesus healed her daughter (Mark 7:24-30). Sickness can't stay when we are under His shade.

In Psalm 119:103 the psalmist says, *"How sweet are your promises to my taste, more than honey to my mouth!"* The bride said, *"His fruit was sweet to my taste"*. The fruit, about which the bride and the psalmist are talking, is His word. The bride shares the experience of staying in the presence of God and the sweetness of His Word, David had the same experience in Psalm 19 and this could be the experience of every member of the church.

Psalm 19:7-10

Yahweh's law is perfect, restoring the soul. Yahweh's covenant is sure, making wise the simple. Yahweh's precepts are right, rejoicing the heart. Yahweh's commandment is pure, enlightening the eyes. The fear of Yahweh is clean, enduring forever. Yahweh's ordinances are true, and righteous altogether. They are more to be desired than gold, yes, than much fine gold, sweeter also than honey and the extract of the honeycomb.

2:4

He brought me to the banquet hall. His banner over me is love.

Jesus led the bride to the banquet hall. Jesus doesn't have favoritism for anyone (Romans 2:11). It is an honor for the guest if the owner of the house personally comes out and leads the guest into the banquet hall. This thing is only done for the people whom you love or have a lot of respect. To His bride, Jesus has both love and respect. Anyone who accepts Christ as his savior becomes a member of His church from any tribe and nation. Jesus has invited people from all over the world. It is an open invitation for everyone.

Colossians 3:1 says, *"... Christ is, seated on the right hand of God"*. When people were about to stone Stephen it is written in Acts 7:56, *"Behold, I see the heavens opened, and the Son of Man standing at the right hand of God!* In Colossians, Paul said that Jesus is sitting at the right hand of God but Acts 7:56 says that Jesus is standing at the right hand of God. Now the question is, whether Jesus is standing or sitting at the right hand of God? The answer is that both the statements written about Jesus are correct. When Jesus rose from the dead, He was seated at the right hand of God; but Stephen saw Jesus standing at the right hand because Stephen was about to die and Jesus was standing to receive His spirit with honor. This was the honor Jesus was giving him. God honors those who are honored by Jesus. Jesus encouraged His disciples to seek the respect which is from God (John 12:43). Stephen was the first martyr from the church and Jesus welcomed him to the banquet hall. Jesus said, *"If anyone serves me, let him follow me. Where I am, there my servant will also be. If anyone serves me, the Father will honor him."* (John 12:26).

The bride is honored by God and Jesus that's why we see a banner over the bride. When soldiers used to come back from the battlefield, they would raise their flags. This was the sign of their victory, and proof that they belong to the kingdom and city they are approaching. The guard opens the gates for them and city people welcome them with cheers and greetings. In the same way, when the bride was brought to the banquet hall, the flag of Jesus was over her. This was the banner of Christ's love. It shows His ownership and His respect for His bride. Jesus loves and honors His bride. Therefore He brings His people home with love and affection. His banner is over us so that the whole world may know that His mercies upon us are beyond measure. It is not because of our good works but because of His everlasting love.

2:5

Strengthen me with raisins, refresh me with apples; for I am faint with love.

The love of Christ is like a wine, the more we take it the more we like it. It is stronger than the desire for money, kingdom, or any other thing of this world. This is why believers preferred death over life without Christ. Up till now thousands of people have accepted death instead of changing their religion because His love is stronger than death. Whether His people go through water or fire, every time the world will hear these words, *"we will not serve your gods or worship the golden image which you have set up* (Daniel 3:18)".

Jesus is represented as an apple tree in this chapter. In Song of Songs 2:3, the bride said that she is sitting under the shade of an apple tree and she likes to eat its fruit. It means she loves Jesus so much that she wants every bit of Him. She is in love with Jesus, He is an apple tree for her, and out of Him, she is gaining strength because she is eating the apple. But, what we can eat and drink from Christ? It is the flesh and blood of Christ.

Matthew 26:26

As they were eating, Jesus took bread, gave thanks for it, and broke it. He gave to the disciples and said, "Take, eat; this is my body."

Song of Songs was written hundreds of years before Christ but it was showing us how Jesus would die. Right from the first book of the Bible, in Genesis 6:3 God said, *"My Spirit will not strive with man forever"*. God started showing that He loves His creation so much that He will send His only son to save us. In Genesis 3:13-19, God punished Adam, Eve, and the Serpent for their sin. While pronouncing their punishment God said, *"I will put hostility between you and the woman, and between your offspring and her offspring. He will bruise your head, and you will bruise his heel."* (Genesis 3:15).

Although God was punishing Adam and Eve, still He didn't forget His mercy. He pronounced the salvation of humanity at the same time as when He pronounced judgment on Adam and Eve. Similarly, in Genesis chapter six, when God decided to punish the whole earth for their sin; God said, *"My Spirit will not strive with man forever".* God punished the people because their works were against His spirit. But, at the same time, He promised that His spirit will live with humans. This promise was fulfilled on the Day of Pentecost in the upper room. So God remembers His mercy even when He is angry. In His love He allowed His body to be torn and provided for us. His body is like an apple, we all are partakers of this apple, which is His flesh. The church is refreshed by the flesh which we take in the form of Holy Communion in the church.

The bride talked about two things. One is an apple and the other is raisin. Raisins are the dried form of grapes. Grapes and raisins had their different uses. Fresh grapes were to be used within a few days of harvesting, whereas raisins were able to be stored for a long time. For us, Jesus acts as both grapes and raisins. Similarly, Old Testament sacrifices lasted for a short period, like fresh grapes but the New Testament focuses on the sacrifice of Jesus which is like raisins which will last for a long time, till eternity. Leviticus 7:17-18, *"but what remains of the meat of the sacrifice on the third day shall be burned with fire. If any of the meat of the sacrifice of his peace offerings is eaten on the third day, it will not be accepted, and it shall not be credited to him who offers it. It will be an abomination, and the soul who eats any of it will bear his iniquity."* By this order of God to use the flesh of the sacrifice within a specific number of days and by burning the leftover meat in the fire, we learn that the sacrifices of old are only for a short time, like fresh grapes. But by reading Revelation 5:12 we see the greatness of Jesus' sacrifice.

Revelation 5:12,

Saying with a loud voice, "Worthy is the Lamb who has been killed to receive the power, wealth, wisdom, strength, honor, glory, and blessing!"

We see that the sacrifice of Jesus will never lose its value, even in eternity. It has not lost its importance for 2000 years and it will never be old. Like raisins, it will have a long, profound effect. So the image of Jesus' sacrifice in the Old Testament was like grapes by which Israel got refreshed, and His sacrifice in the New Testament refreshes the present-day church like raisins.

Grape juice is good for health. As wine was a fermented drink, it was not permitted for use during the days of the Passover festival, only fresh grape juice was allowed in those days (Exodus 12:15-39, 13:1-7). Jesus initiated Holy Communion on the Day of Passover. So it was not fermented wine which Jesus took on that occasion. Jesus' body was bruised. His blood was coming out of His body like someone is treading fresh grapes in the winepress. The blood of Jesus saves us and protects us from evil. Jesus represented the fresh grape juice with His blood (Matthew 26:27-28). The bride said, *"Strengthen me with raisins"*. Cakes of raisins were used to save the dried raisins in the form of cakes. These cakes were usually given to army men and people who go on long journeys so that they could use it at the time of need (1-Samuel 30:12, 2-Samuel 6:19). The word of Jesus is like raisins which remain nourishing for a long time and keep on refreshing our soul. The bride of Christ is refreshed by the visitation of Christ as an apple and gets strength by His word as people get strength by eating raisin cakes. His sacrifice also shows the same concept of grapes and raisins in the Old and New Testament.

2:6

His left hand is under my head. His right hand embraces me.

People on the left and right side of a king show closeness of relationship and the king's trust in the people. The closest person usually stood on the right side of the person with authority. The eldest son, or the son whom father loves the most, used to stand on the right side of the father. In Mark 10:35-37 it is written, *James and John, the sons of Zebedee, came near to him, saying, "Teacher, we want you to do for us whatever we will ask." He said to them, "What do you want me to do for you?" They said to him, "Grant to us that we may sit, one at your right hand, and one at your left hand, in your glory."*

By requesting of Jesus a place at His left and right, they were requesting Jesus to be His closest companion in His glory. They wanted to be treated as the highest-ranking officers in His kingdom. Some people thought that Jesus' kingdom would be on this earth, that He would fight the Romans and give the kingdom to the Israelites. These two disciples had the same kind of thoughts.

This verse shows the intimacy between the bride and bridegroom, but there are other lessons as well. The bride said that Christ is using both of His hands to bring her near to Him. Jesus is esteeming her very high because the position on the right and left show the seat of honor. While bringing her closer, He is holding her head with His left hand. Holding someone's head high means you desire honor for that person. Jesus is supporting the head of the bride. It is only by His support that we are recognized with honor in this world. This world says many bad things about Christians but when they talk about modesty, helping the poor, honesty, and other social values, they will look towards the church because you will not find such great values anywhere else. Some people are very good to other people but if other people oppose them, they will answer them with the same attitude; whereas Christ taught His bride to do good even to your enemies (Matthew 5:44-46). There are religions where we see that the leader killed others to save himself or his people. Jesus didn't put anyone to death, neither to save himself nor to save his people. Instead, He had been raising people from the dead and healing His enemies even when they came to arrest him in the garden of Gethsemane (Luke 22:49-51). While others were taking His life, He forgave them (Luke 23:34). We don't see such patience and teaching anywhere else. These are the ideals Jesus practically taught us, and His people are applying His teaching everywhere. As Jesus taught us these things; by teaching us the best values, He holds our head high with His hand.

He uses His right arm to embrace us. It means He is the one who brings us closer to Him. Our efforts are worthless. *For we have all become like one who is unclean, and all our righteousness is like a polluted garment* (Isaiah 64:6). In Luke 7:36-50, Jesus was invited by a Pharisee to have dinner at his home. While they were having dinner a woman who was considered as a sinner, came into the house. She kissed Jesus' feet a lot, poured oil on His head and perfume on His feet. The Pharisee was troubled by the fact that the woman was a sinner and Jesus was not stopping her from touching Him. The Pharisee thought poorly of Jesus. To explain the woman's position, Jesus told a parable to the Pharisee. He said if there are two sinners and God forgives both of them then the sinner who had more sins would be more thankful. In this way, the woman who was considered as the worst sinner was forgiven, and she showed more love than the Pharisee. Jesus was showing the Pharisee that she is not the only sinner. The Pharisee was a sinner as well; and both of them need salvation. These were not the works of the Pharisee or the woman; it was by the grace of Jesus that they both came to salvation. Jesus allowed them to enter His kingdom by gaining forgiveness for their sins. In this way, Jesus was embracing them. He was welcoming them home by extending His right arm towards them with dignity and honor.

2:7

I adjure you, daughters of Jerusalem, by the roes, or by the hinds of the field, that you not stir up, nor awaken love, until it so desires.

The Daughters of Jerusalem are believers from different nations. In Luke 23:28 it is written, *But Jesus, turning to them, said, "Daughters of Jerusalem, don't weep for me, but weep for yourselves and for your children.* Jesus was addressing the faithful women but those women were not from Jerusalem. They were from Galilee and had been serving Jesus in Galilee. The time when Jesus was crucified was the time of the Passover festival. These women came from Galilee to be with Jesus during the festival (Mark 15:40-41). But, why was Jesus calling the ladies from Galilee Daughters of Jerusalem? Why didn't he call them Daughters of Galilee? Because "Daughters of Jerusalem" is the term used for believers. In the Bible the word "daughters" is symbolically used for nations; Psalm 48:11, 97:8, Isaiah 16:2, and Ezekiel 16:46 used the word "daughters", symbolically for nations. Galatians 4:26 calls Jerusalem the mother of believers; *"But the Jerusalem that is above is free, which is the mother of us all"*. This verse is for all the believers in different nations. Jerusalem is called the mother of believers because this is the place where the birth of the church took place. From Jerusalem, believers spread all over the world and preached the gospel. In different countries, if there were any theological problems, they used to consult with the apostles in Jerusalem (Acts 15:1-35), as children come to their mother to settle their issues. The church in Jerusalem used to monitor the activities of different churches and apostles (Acts 11:22-24). The church elders in Jerusalem took care of the daughter churches in different parts of their own country and the world as would a mother. Therefore Jerusalem is known as the mother of believers and believers are known as "Daughters of Jerusalem".

The bride charged the women of Jerusalem by the gazelles and does. Gazelles and does were considered as clean animals which were allowed to be eaten (Deuteronomy 12:15). Gazelles are very beautiful animals. They are the beauties of the jungle. They are part of the food chain among wild animals. They can run for long distances. They are highly alert and sensitive to the presence of other animals; this helps in saving them from predators. They like to live in herds. King David compared deer/gazelle (biologically they are from the same family) with a believer (Psalm 42:1, 2-Samuel 22:34). God helps believers to remain safe from the attacks of the devil. It is by His strength that we may run like a deer and save our life (Habakkuk 3:19). One of the characteristics described by King David is that a deer longs for the water brooks (Psalm 42:1). David spent a long time in the jungles. He had been observing animals there. He knew that deer ran fast for long distances. After this, water becomes necessary to keep them alive. Water becomes their utmost desire. David relates that desire for water with a believer's desire for God's presence. In this way, in this verse of Song of Songs, a deer represents a believer.

When the bride charged the daughters of Jerusalem by gazelles, she was giving them a vow by other believers. To awake the bridegroom irrespective of His desire means to do works against His will. When someone breaks a vow, he will be hurting the person by whom he vowed. When you are charged by someone, it means that person would die if you break the vow. As the bride has charged the daughters of Jerusalem by gazelles; and gazelles/ deer represents believers, it means if you will be going against the will of the bridegroom or commandments of Jesus Christ, you will hurt other believers. There are times when our actions bring shame to other believers. There are times when our actions bring disrepute upon other believers. These are the times when we are going against the will of the bridegroom. If we misbehave with someone or take part in illegal activities, worldly people will think that other Christians behave in the same way. In this way, we will be hurting the dignity of the church. We should think carefully before doing something to ensure our actions may not go against the body of Christ.

2:8

The voice of my beloved! Behold, he comes, leaping on the mountains, skipping on the hills.

Mountains and hills in this verse represent obstacles between us and Jesus. When Adam and Eve were in Eden, Satan did his best to create a hindrance between them and God. God announced in the Garden of Eden that He would send a deliverer through a woman. Later Satan tried to bring corruption among women. In Genesis 6:1-2 it is written, *"When men began to multiply on the surface of the ground, and daughters were born to them, God's sons saw that men's daughters were beautiful, and they took any that they wanted for themselves as wives".* Many Bible teachers teach that the term "God's sons or sons of God" is used for the fallen angels. In Job 38:4-7 it is written,

Where were you when I laid the foundations of the earth? Declare, if you have understanding. Who determined its measures, if you know? Or who stretched the line on it? What were its foundations fastened on? Or who laid its cornerstone, when the morning stars sang together, and all the sons of God shouted for joy?

God is talking about the time before the creation of man. Angels were created before the human beings and they were happy seeing the wonders of God every day; because every day God was doing something new (Genesis Chapter 1). They were praising God and shouting with joy. In the NIV, the word "angels" is used but some other translations, and in Hebrew, instead of "angels" the word "the sons of God" is used. So "sons of God" and "angels" are used interchangeably. Therefore, it is a general perception about Genesis 6:1-2 that fallen angels took the ladies in the days of Noah, and through this combination, Nephilim were born on earth. Eventually, God bought the great flood on the earth. He saved Noah and his family to continue the human race and bring salvation through

Noah's descendants. God foiled the plan of Satan to hinder salvation; Jesus crossed that hill to save His people.

God promised Abraham that He will bless the whole world through him (Genesis Chapter 12). In the time of Noah, Satan targeted the whole world because he didn't know which lady will be used by God to bring salvation on the earth. Now he had a specific target, and that was Abraham. In Genesis Chapter 3, God promised that the savior will come through a woman. So now he targeted Abraham's wife. Abraham's wife, Sara was taken by Pharaoh to be his wife. Satan wanted to bring corruption in Sara's life through Pharaoh but God rescued Sara from Pharaoh's palace (Genesis 12:14-20). When Satan failed in Abraham's life, he targeted his son's life. Isaac's wife was in danger that someone from the people of king Abimelek of Gerar would marry her, although she was already married to Isaac (Genesis 26:7-11). Another obstacle created by Satan in Isaac's life was the bareness of Rebecca. Satan didn't want Isaac's descendants to come into this world and then bring the savior Jesus to the earth. Isaac prayed for this situation and God again intervened to heal her (Genesis 25:21). In this way every time Satan tried to bring mountains of problems, Jesus crossed them to reach His people. No one can keep Him away from His people.

When someone is on one side of a hill or mountain and you are on the other side then you can't see or hear each other because of the distance in between. The bridegroom is not near the bride, but she can hear Him. Not only is she hearing Him; she is trying to encourage others to also listen to her beloved. She can identify the moves of the bridegroom; that He is leaping across the mountains and bounding over the hills. These descriptions show the spiritual discernment that the bride has. She is not able to see the bridegroom with her natural eyes but her spirit is so in tune with the Holy Spirit that she can understand the movements of the bridegroom.

When we grow in Spirit and relationship with Christ, we start understanding even the non-verbal communication with our friend, Jesus Christ. We begin to know His desire even without His speech.

He wants a peak in our relationship where words don't matter anymore. Moses had that kind of relationship with God. On Mount Sinai, God said that he would destroy the Israelites but Moses knew God's heart is full of mercy, and it's not the heart desire of God to destroy His people. Moses interceded for the Israelites and God forgave them. In this incident, God was angry with the Israelites and wanted to punish them. But Moses knew the depth of God's heart, and that God was grieved for His people. Moses knew this because he used to spend quality time with God. He had recently spent forty days and nights with God. He received the pattern for the Tabernacle, and the Law for the Israelites. Why would God give him the Law if God's heart wasn't knitted with the Israelites? God wanted to live with His people (Exodus 25:8) and those laws were the guidelines so that His people would know the way to live with God. Moses knew that all those revelations were given by God because of the love God had for Israel. God wanted to develop an intimacy between Himself and His people. God wanted that intimacy with living people, not with dead ones. Moses knew that it's the right of God to be angry with His people because they left Him and went after an idol. People broke the covenant they made with God. In ancient times, if there was a covenant between two parties and one of the parties broke the covenant then the penalty was death. So God was right when He said that He would destroy the Israelites. Moses knew another truth; that although God is angry with His people, His heart is still filled with love and compassion for His people. It is the same scenario when a mother wants to discipline her children with punishment, but her heart is full of love for her children. Verbally God was saying that He wanted to punish Israel, but Moses was able to hear the heartbeat of God which was saying that I am deeply grieved about my people. Moses was known as a friend of God (Exodus 33:11). Being the bride of Christ, we also need such a friendship; to be very close to God to hear Him. This kind of understanding can be developed by the experience of staying in the presence of God. This is why Paul said, *"Don't be conformed to this world, but be transformed by the renewing of your mind, so that you may prove what is the good, well-pleasing, and perfect will of God."* (Romans 12:2). When we have intimacy with God, we are able to tell others that my beloved, my Christ is coming. None of the mountains, hills, or any other obstacle could stop Him.

2:9

My beloved is like a roe or a young deer. Behold, he stands behind our wall! He looks in at the windows. He glances through the lattice.

In the previous verse, we saw that the beloved Christ was coming, crossing all the obstacles in His way. In this verse, we see that He reached the house of the bride. He is like a deer that runs very fast but when he reaches His desired beloved, He does not enter the house. He does this because he respects our free will. He is standing beside the wall and He is doing two things. He is showing himself through the lattice. The view through a lattice is not clear. It means the viewpoint or perspective of the bride is not clear about Him but He can see the bride clearly because He is gazing through the openings. We can't see Him fully because of the bars of lattice in between us and Him. *For now we see in a mirror, dimly, but then face to face. Now I know in part, but then I will know fully, even as I was also fully known* (1-Corinthians 13:12). We are body and He is Spirit. We can't comprehend Him fully with our human mind; but because of the love he has for us, He wants us to know Him completely. To fulfill this desire, He has given us His Spirit to live in us. *But you are not in the flesh but in the Spirit, if it is so that the Spirit of God dwells in you. But if any man doesn't have the Spirit of Christ, he is not his* (Romans 8:9).

Whilst we are in this body there is a wall between us and Him, and He is standing on the other side of the wall. There could be different walls between us and Him. In Mark 10:17-23, we see a rich man who loved his riches very much. He also wanted to get salvation. Jesus told him to sell everything he had and give it to the poor. To have money is not a sin but to love money more than God is a sin. Therefore Jesus told him to give away that thing which is causing sin for him but he didn't want to do this. The riches had become a wall between him and God. This wall needed to be demolished by the rich man, not by God. Jesus didn't cross that wall because salvation is a gift and God doesn't give it forcefully. So He shows us the wall in between our relationship with God and He stands on the other side of the wall and eagerly watches so that He may embrace us as soon as we break down that wall.

There was a Pharisee named Nicodemus (John 3:1-12). He came to Jesus at night and Jesus told him about the new birth. It was difficult for him to understand. He came at night because he was afraid of Jews. His fear was a wall between him and Jesus. Able was angry with his brother, Cain. God told Able to cast away the anger from his heart. He didn't listen to God. In his anger, he killed his brother. So his anger built a wall between him and God. Because of our shortcomings, we keep on closing the space in the window, through which we might see God. We keep on adding the bars of sin and doubt to convert the window into a lattice. We try to see God through that lattice but the bars of the lattice hinder our full view of Jesus. Different people try to see Jesus through their lattice and they count the sacrifice of Jesus as foolishness. They read the Old Testament and see the punishment given by God to discipline His people as cruelty. They are not able to see the love behind that discipline because of the bars of their lattice they have created with their prejudice. God disciplines us because He loves us (Hebrews 12:4-11).

We look at Him through our lattice, but He looks at us through the window. Because of His clarity of vision, He doesn't have any doubt about us. He can see into the hearts and minds of people. When Peter came to Jesus to talk about the temple tax, even before Peter said anything to Him, He knew that Peter wanted to talk about the tax payment. He told Peter to go and fish; and get a coin from a fish's mouth to pay the tax (Matthew 17:24-26). Gideon was depressed about himself but God called him a "mighty man". He was hiding himself and his possessions, but God looked into his heart and saw a leader there. He has a clear picture of every one of us. Let's have as clear a vision of Him as he has of us.

John 2:23-25

Now when he was in Jerusalem at the Passover, during the feast, many believed in his name, observing his signs which he did. But Jesus didn't entrust himself to them, because he knew everyone, and because he didn't need for anyone to testify concerning man; for he himself knew what was in man.

2:10

My beloved spoke, and said to me, "Rise up, my love, my beautiful one, and come away.

The bridegroom asked the bride to arise and come with Him. Spiritually we have two stages in life. In stage one we arise in response to the speech of Christ and in stage two we walk after Him. If He orders, nobody dares to disobey Him; even the dead listened and obeyed Him. He ordered Lazarus to come out of the grave; Lazarus rose from the dead and came out of the grave. He commanded diseases and they left people. None of the demons dares to stand against His command but when it is the turn of His bride, He doesn't command her, and He talks with her and leaves it to her choice to obey or not, because He doesn't force humans.

When going to heaven Jesus commanded his disciples to make disciples in other nations. The church at that time took it as a great commission and spread the Word of God in the world, but the present-day church is not taking it seriously. God is not judging the people immediately, but a day will come when we have to stand before the judgment throne of Christ. When Jesus was crucified, some ladies were weeping for Jesus. Jesus told them not to weep for Him but their children. In Luke 10:13-15, Jesus prophesied against different cities in Israel. This was the signal that great destruction was on the way to Israel. When Jesus told the women to weep for their children, He was referring to the prophecy He spoke in Luke 10:13-15. Jesus said the same thing again and again; first to all the Israel in Luke 10:13-15 and then specifically to the church. The church could choose whether they would rise in prayer to save their children or not. Jesus didn't force them to obey Him but there are consequences associated with obeying or disobeying the command. We can see Jesus prophesying against the cities who didn't accept Him in Matthew 11:20-24. History shows that the church gave value to what Jesus told them about the destruction which was coming and left their cities, but the Israelites didn't give ear to His warnings; so many Israelites were murdered by the Romans in 70 AD. Being the bride of Christ, we need to obey Him. If he is asking us to come after him, we need to go.

2:11

For behold, the winter is past. The rain is over and gone.

Winter is the hard season for most people. Some animals like bears and frogs hide in safe places during winter. Paul used to spend winter someplace with church people in order to strengthen them, and in summer he would go to different places to evangelize other people (1-Corinthians 16:6, Titus 3:12). Spiritually speaking, the time in the Old Testament was the time of winter. At that time the Good News was limited to one nation, Israel. The Israelites felt proud because they thought that salvation belongs only to them. They thought that other nations were unholy and Jews shouldn't eat or mingle with them (Acts 10:28). It wasn't God who restricted

Himself only to the Israelites, it was the beliefs of the Israelites. Our God is the God of Nations (Psalm 86:9, 2-Samuel 22:50, Isaiah 19:18-25). The Gentiles' time of waiting is over now, for them the winter is over. They can freely come to God and get salvation through faith. *For there is no distinction between Jew and Greek; for the same Lord is Lord of all, and is rich to all who call on him. For, "Whoever will call on the name of the Lord will be saved."* (Romans 10:12-13).

Jesus is encouraging His bride to come with Him because winter is past and summer is starting. Since the time when the fire of the Holy Spirit fell on the disciples, the spiritual summer has started for the church. The church has to serve God by reaching others with the gospel. The rain in winter was a blessing. It helped the crops to grow. In Joel 2:23, God promised former and latter rain. Former rain is already sent by God and after this, we have seen an abundance of spiritual crops in the history of mankind. Jesus knew this was going to happen. Therefore He said, *"The harvest indeed is plentiful, but the laborers are few. Pray therefore that the Lord of the harvest will send out laborers into his harvest"* (Matthew 9:37-38). Jesus wants more and more people to work in His orchard (Matthew 20:1-16). Therefore He encouraged His bride to step out in the mission field because He has made everything ready for her, everything needed for evangelism.

2:12

The flowers appear on the earth. The time of the singing has come, and the voice of the turtledove is heard in our land.

In Song of Songs, the place named, "Lebanon" is used again and again. Solomon had a palace in Lebanon so perhaps when Song of Songs was written, he could have been staying in that palace. In that area, there is snow in winter. In winter during the snowy season, we usually don't see any growth on the ground. When spring comes, we see a lot of activities on earth. We see flowers blooming; birds singing and animals are in a happy mood. Flowers are for two things; either they are just for beauty and fragrance or they give the promise of the new crop when we see them on the fruit trees. The bridegroom calls his bride as a dove. He is referring to the doves in the field; He can hear their voice. After winter, there is a short time for spring and then there is summer. Mostly doves lay eggs in summer and in this way they bring up a new generation of doves in this world.

Fruitful trees often represent faithful people in the church (Psalm 1:1-3). Jesus is telling His church that everything in nature is ready to reproduce something of their kind. So the church should also reproduce and start working for new daughter churches; help those churches in reaching the stage of maturity and those daughter churches should repeat the same process of reproduction. The springtime which is described in this verse is a beautiful time but it is also full of dangers. As soon as new flowers start emerging, different insects/ diseases also start coming and target the new crops. These insects sometimes help in the growth with pollination but sometimes they destroy the whole crop. The new crop from beginning to end needs a lot of care. We need to examine the plants regularly. The same is true with our kids at home and people in the church. We need to observe that our kids do not have such friends or activities which can destroy them or their fruit. Paul labored a lot for the people among whom he was serving. When we read Galatians 4:17-20, we see that the Church of Galatia was going through a spiritual problem. They were having fellowship with people who looked like their friends, but were destroying them slowly and secretly. Galatians 4:8-11 shows that they were going back to idolatry. They were adopting rituals which were not beneficial for them. Paul said, *"My little children, of whom I am again in travail until Christ is formed in you"* (Gal 4:19). After gaining salvation, it is not wise that we may stay as we are, we need to imitate Jesus until we become like Jesus. *Don't be conformed to this world, but be transformed by the renewing of your mind* (Romans 12:2). Our minds need to be transformed.

This is an internal change whose effects can be seen in our outward behavior. It is not an easy or instantaneous process. It is a lifelong continuous process. When we keep on changing our inner being, we keep on growing in His glory (2-Corinthians 3:18). Paul worked hard for the salvation of people in Galatia. His efforts worked well; they accepted Christ. Now they were again interested in their old life. If they went back to idolatry, it would be a waste of the time, energy, and efforts of Paul; they would be wasting the mercy of God on their lives. Paul again started interceding for them; as he was doing when they had not accepted Christ. Therefore Paul said*, "My little children, of whom I am again in travail until Christ is formed in you"* (Galatians 4:19).

We may see ourselves in a new season of church growth but we need to take care of our older partners as well. We should be careful in this time of spring that we not lose souls we won for Christ previously. It is a time for Christ's dove to come out and be involved in raising new chicks, but we need to be careful because new helpless chicks are often easy prey for snakes and other predators. We need to remain on guard against the old serpent who tries to devour God's people.

It is a time of singing because when we sing praises of our God, God's anointing rests on His people. It is through the anointing that the yoke is broken. Spiritually, it is springtime. We need to come out and preach the gospel but it is not possible until we have God on our side. Our God rejoices with us when we worship Him and He stands with His people. When He stands with us, nobody can stand against us. The good news is not just the words. While preaching the gospel, Jesus always healed people. Good news is the news about Jesus; news about deliverance from sins and healing from diseases. Healing and deliverance come through anointing and anointing comes through singing and worship which arises from the heart. When His dove opens its mouth to worship, He rejoices over us.

2:13

The fig tree ripens her green figs. The vines are in blossom. They give out their fragrance. Arise, my love, my beautiful one, and come away."

The fig tree forms its early fruit; the blossoming vines spread their fragrance. In the Bible, fig tree leaves were first used by Adam and Eve to cover themselves (Genesis 3:7). Figs were not only used as fresh fruit; they can be dried for later use. Figs also had some medicinal properties to heal boils (2-Kings 20:7). Fruitful trees like the fig and the vine are used to bring joy to people through their fruit (Joel 1:12). Many times when God became angry with the Israelites, He struck their fruit trees. Amos 4:9 says, *"I struck you with blight and mildew many times in your gardens and your vineyards; and the swarming locusts have devoured your fig trees and your olive trees; yet you haven't returned to me," says Yahweh.* The fig tree and vine are often mentioned together in the Bible. They symbolize peace and prosperity. When peace and prosperity were being discussed in the era of Solomon; it is written, *"Judah and Israel lived safely, every man under his vine and under his fig tree, from Dan even to Beersheba, all the days of Solomon"* (1-Kings 4:25).

Jesus tells His bride that the fig tree is bringing its fruit and the vine is ready to give its fruit as well. In every season when fresh fruits start to come into the market, the price rises but when the same fruit is abundant in the market the price goes down. The first fruits in any season are the fruits which come on the branches at the start of the fruit season. Through these first fruits, the Israelites were to worship their God.

You shall take some of the first of all the fruit of the ground, which you shall bring in from your land that Yahweh your God gives you. You shall put it in a basket, and shall go to the place which Yahweh your God shall choose to cause his name to dwell there (Deuteronomy 26:2).

Jesus is telling His bride that the time to get the first fruit has come. Paul called the first converts in an area, the first fruits of that area. *Now I beg you, brothers—you know the house of Stephanas, that it is the first fruits of Achaia, and that they have set themselves to serve the saints* (1-Corinthians 16:15). Jesus is encouraging the church to be ready to receive the first fruits. The first fruits or first converts from different parts of the world. Priests were to receive the first fruits. There were proper storage places for articles the Israelites used to bring as offerings. The big question for the church today is, "do we have good storage places for the first fruits of souls we will receive?" If we don't have the storage places, proper ministries to take care of new believers, then we can lose those souls. Today this could be one of the reasons that we have less attendance in the churches and slowly churches are becoming empty. By mentioning the early fruits of fig trees and vines, Jesus is encouraging His church to be ready for the new people in the church. We need Jesus to lead us in this process. He is the only one who can train us to be the fishers of men (Matthew 4:19). That is why He was asking the bride to come with Him.

2:14

My dove in the clefts of the rock, in the hiding places of the mountainside, let me see your face. Let me hear your voice; for your voice is sweet and your face is lovely.

A cliff is a strong place to live ~~in~~. Jesus is the strongest rock on which our house is built. If any storm will come, our rock will save us. *Yahweh is my rock, my fortress, and my deliverer; my God, my rock, in whom I take refuge; my shield, and the horn of my salvation, my high tower* (Psalm 18:2). This world is a battlefield in which we are constantly fighting against the forces of darkness. That is why in 2-Corinthians 10:4-5, Paul talked about the weapons of our warfare; "*for the weapons of our warfare are not of the flesh, but mighty before God to the throwing down of strongholds, throwing down imaginations and every high thing that is exalted against the knowledge of God and bringing every thought into captivity to the obedience of Christ"*. Often on the battlefield, the army who has its position on the rock has more advantages as compared to that which is in the valley. Our God is our rock. Our weapons are better, and being on the rock, we are in a better position. To target the enemies' hidden positions, He has given us spiritual ears and eyes. The King of Aram was an enemy of Israel. He makes plans against Israel (2-Kings 6:8-11) but God kept on revealing those plans to Elijah and Elijah told those things to the Israelite king. God proves Himself mighty all the time.

Sometimes we just want to live on the rock safely and we don't want to participate in the work for which we are in this world. We don't want to leave our comfort zone. God wants us to come out of our small nest or small thinking. We become so focused on our own goals that we stop thinking about God. We stop reading the Word and praying to God; which is the main source of communication with God. Therefore He said, "*let me see your face. Let me hear your voice"*. Being a father, he desires to stay in touch with us. The father of the prodigal son desired to see his face and hear his voice. That is why every day the father used to keep on looking at the road from where his son was expected to come. One day the father saw him from far and ran towards him (Luke 15:11-24). It was not the son who ran to the father, but the father ran to him. The father had been waiting for this moment a long time. The same desire is expressed in this verse of Song of Songs. Our bridegroom is waiting for us.

When we speak under the anointing then there will be power from above in those words. Listeners will be blessed, healed, and grown in Christ. Jesus is calling His church, His dove to come out. When the first time his dove came out, a great revival was seen in Israel. Three thousand men accepted Christ as a result of a single speech of Simon (Acts 2:41). Demon possessed and all kinds of sick people were healed just by the shadow of Peter (Acts 5:15). Jesus wants His bride to come out with the same zeal and power in all ages. The church doesn't need the world, the world needs the church.

Jesus is the head of the Church and we are His body. When He was on this earth, people used to touch His body and were healed from their sicknesses. Today the world is waiting for the church to rise so that world can be healed of its problems. *For the creation waits with eager expectation for the children of God to be revealed* (Romans 8:19). Jesus indeed loves His church and that's why He is calling it, but there is another truth as well; He loves the lost world and wants to save it by sending believers into the world.

2:15

Catch for us the foxes, the little foxes that plunder the vineyards; for our vineyards are in blossom.

Jesus is commanding His workers to catch the foxes to save the vineyard, but who are these workers? Before going into further details let's find out something about these workers in the Old and New Testament. In the Old Testament, we see three main ministries in Israel. These were the King, prophet, and priest. Their duty in Israel was to lead the Israelites according to the Law given through Moses. In the New Testament, we see a fivefold ministry. *He gave some to be apostles; and some, prophets; and some, evangelists; and some, shepherds and teachers; for the perfecting of the saints, to the work of serving, to the building up of the body of Christ, until we all attain to the unity of the faith and of the knowledge of the Son of God, to a full grown man, to the measure of the stature of the fullness of Christ* (Ephesians 4:11-13). According to these verses, all of these five ministries are initiated by Christ to help the church in spiritual growth. But we see they don't work only in the church but they have some work outside the church. Out of these five ministries, three are usually seen working in the local church. These three are pastors, teachers, and prophets. Out of the remaining two, an evangelist has to go to other churches and strengthen them by preaching or staying there for some time. Whereas an apostle's main work is among gentiles, although it is a duty of every one of us to reach the unreached people and share the gospel with them. But, as apostles and evangelists mostly work outside the local church, so they must collect the fruit in the form of saved spirits; bring them to the local church, and then the duty of the pastors, prophets, and teachers starts from there to help them in growing in Christ.

This fivefold ministry is responsible for harvesting and taking care of the fruit. While taking care of the fruit, we need to keep it safe from various diseases. But at the same time, we need to keep the harvest safe from different birds and animals. The bride specifically talked about small and fully-grown foxes. Foxes are considered a very clever animal. According to an estimation, the per annum loss due to foxes in vineyards in different parts of the world is millions of dollars. They dig holes under the earth near vineyards; take rest during the day and attack in the darkness of night. Sometimes they destroy the whole crop of the season. If they make holes near the roots, it can destroy the vine. These holes make the root system weak and the vine wouldn't be able to get the proper nourishment, which could lessen the yield of the vine. Farmers need to keep on searching for the holes or dens made by foxes.

To drive away or capture the foxes, farmers need to be on guard at night and patrol during the day to find and close down the holes made by foxes. Like foxes, Satan and his agents come in the darkness. We need God's glory to illuminate our ways through His Word because His Word is a lamp unto our feet (Psalm 119:105). Jesus said that the enemy came at night to sow weeds among the wheat (Matthew 13:25). Jesus usually spent nights in prayer. In prayer, God reveals His will and plans of the enemy (1-Samuel 23:11). Satan used Judas as a fox to destroy the vines Jesus planted as His disciples. God revealed to Jesus that Satan was going to attack Him and His disciples on the night before the crucifixion. Therefore He told His disciples to stay awake and pray. In Matthew 26:38 He said, *"Stay here and watch with me"*; then in Matthew 26:41, He said, *"Watch and pray, that you don't enter into temptation"*. Satan was bringing temptation and the way to defeat him was through prayer. First Jesus said, *"Watch"* and then He said, *"Watch and pray"*. You can't guard or watch His flock without prayer. Through prayer, you can activate the ministry of angels to fight the forces of darkness trying to enter your vineyard. At the beginning of His ministry, Jesus stayed in prayer and fasting for forty days. Satan tempted Jesus, but He remained strong in temptation through prayer and He rebutted him through the Word of God. Satan wanted to stop Him from entering His ministry. At the end of Jesus' earthly ministry, Satan wanted to destroy everything He did, along with His disciples; therefore he was asking His disciples to stay awake and pray with Him.

The bride talked about the small and big foxes because enemies can come in any form; even in the form of your church members. The enemy came to Eve in the form of a serpent. Everyday Eve had seen a serpent in the garden. So a fox or enemy can come in the form of some familiar face. To Adam, the enemy came in the form of Eve. Satan can use your family members to deceive you. We need to ask God to intervene to protect the flock because He is the chief shepherd and owner of the vineyard (1-Peter 5:4, Isaiah 5:7).

2:16

My beloved is mine, and I am his. He browses among the lilies.

The bride is saying that she belongs to the bridegroom. Jesus is talking about His bride, and that His bride belongs to Him. We should know the one to whom we belong. Sometimes we live a life with double standards. We want to please God but on the other hand, we don't want to leave Satan's party either. If we don't belong to God, we will end up in hell, but if we are living a double-standard life, then we will eliminate our share from the inheritance of believers in heaven. This is very clear from the story of Ananias and Sapphira in Acts Chapter 5. They wanted to be called Christians and at the same time, they wanted to continue their association with

Satan. If we want to say that we belong to Jesus and Jesus belongs to us then we need to make a firm decision to dedicate ourselves totally to God. So that we may boldly say, *"Who shall separate us from the love of Christ? Could oppression, or anguish, or persecution, or famine, or nakedness, or peril, or sword?"* (Romans 8:35) and Jesus may say for each one of us, *"I also tell you that you are Peter, and on this rock I will build my assembly, and the gates of Hades will not prevail against it. I will give to you the keys of the Kingdom of Heaven, and whatever you bind on earth will have been bound in heaven; and whatever you release on earth will have been released in heaven"* (Matthew 16:18-19). The people, who dedicate their lives to Jesus so that no one can separate them from Christ, will get revelations like Peter. Revelations give us a deeper understanding of the written Word, and the church can't stand against Satan without revelations. A church is built on the basis of these revelations. These revelations are the keys to open or close heaven.

Jesus browses his sheep among lilies. In Matthew 6:28-34, Jesus said,

"*Why are you anxious about clothing? Consider the lilies of the field, how they grow. They don't toil, neither do they spin, yet I tell you that even Solomon in all his glory was not dressed like one of these. But if God so clothes the grass of the field, which today exists and tomorrow is thrown into the oven, won't he much more clothe you, you of little faith? "Therefore don't be anxious, saying, 'What will we eat?', 'What will we drink?' or, 'With what will we be clothed?' For the Gentiles seek after all these things; for your heavenly Father knows that you need all these things. But seek first God's Kingdom and his righteousness; and all these things will be given to you as well. Therefore don't be anxious for tomorrow, for tomorrow will be anxious for itself. Each day's own evil is sufficient.*"

Jesus gave the example of a lily and explained that the life of believers should be like lilies. Nobody takes care of wild lilies even then they grow and show their beauty to everyone who looks at them. In their life, there are no worries. One of the main reasons for many mental and physical diseases is worries. We need to work hard and leave the results to God. We should trust in our lives that everything which comes from Him will be in our best interests. If we will keep on trusting Him, we will live a worry-less life. Our worries show our lack of faith in His abilities to fix all the problems and sustain us in all the circumstances of life. By saying that He browses His flock among the lilies, He means that He wants us to learn that we need to trust Him. In Genesis 30:31-43, we see that Jacob used to put the sticks in front of his sheep and goats when they came to drink water. During mating, the sheep and goats were looking at those sticks. Through that technique, he got the offspring as streaked or speckled or spotted, according to his need. The effect of the setting where the sheep had been mating was seen in their offspring. Similarly, Jesus had been taking His sheep in the fields where lilies are grown, that His sheep may see the lilies and they may give birth to other sheep that may grow in faith like lilies. He wants His people to trust God throughout their life. When His sheep or His people have that faith then they will transfer that faith to the new generation of believers who will be born into the kingdom of heaven through believers.

2:17

Until the day is cool, and the shadows flee away, turn, my beloved, and be like a roe or a young deer on the mountains of Bether.

The bride requests the bridegroom to come to her before the night starts. She doesn't want to stay alone during the night. The night or darkness represents problematic times. She doesn't want to call anyone else; she trusts in the Lord, so she is calling Him. In the early days of the church, Stephen was murdered by Jews (Acts 7:7-8, 54-60). After that King Herod started the persecution of Christians. He arrested some Christians and killed Jesus' disciple,

James, the brother of John. Jews were already against Christians. Jews were already against Christians and, knowing they had the support of the State, might have tried to intensify their persecution of Christians; as Haman tried to kill all the Jews in the territory of King Xerxes (Ester 3:5-6). Herod was trying to please the Jews and the Jews wanted Herod's favor by working against Christians. On one side Christianity was growing. On the other side, plans were being made to destroy Christians and their leaders. James was one of the leaders. When Herod saw that it pleased Jews when he killed James, he arrested another leader, Peter (Acts 12:1-19). He wanted to kill Peter as well. By then, the church realized that they were losing all the leaders one by one. It was like the deep darkness of the night. The church was praying like the bride in this verse to come before the night falls. They needed the light of Christ. They started praying. In response to their prayers, angels started working on behalf of the church. God sent an angel who brought Peter out of prison. God foiled the plans of the enemy. As the blood of lambs and goats, which was symbolic of the blood of Christ, stopped the death and Pharaoh's slavery; the prayers of believers stopped the activities of Herod. Sometime later, Herod was in a ceremony; people praised him like he was a god. *Immediately an angel of the Lord struck him, because he didn't give God the glory. Then he was eaten by worms and died* (Acts 12:23). Herod and the Jews were combining their forces; dark shadows were covering the Christians. But when they called upon Christ, they were saved. In the same way, the bride was requesting the bridegroom to stay with her, if a difficult time comes in her life.

The bride requested Christ to be like a gazelle. Gazelles and stags are strong animals that fight to get their mate. They protect their mate from others. They can run very fast for long distances and climb the rugged mountains swiftly. The bride wanted the protection and the closeness of the bridegroom all the time. The church, as the bride, doesn't only want protection through Christ; it is a matter of love and affection that the church has for Christ. The Church wants to be with Jesus in good and bad times. Many believers feel very happy when a whole-night prayer meeting is arranged because they like to spend time with Christ. They feel fresh and empowered after staying in prayer. The love we have for Christ can't be measured by how much we talk about Him but by how much time we spend happily in prayer. Like a bride, we should have the thirst for Christ our bridegroom, to be with Him when darkness comes.

3

3:1

By night on my bed, I sought him whom my soul loves. I sought him, but I didn't find him.

The bride was looking for the bridegroom on the bed but He wasn't in the home. When we love someone more than our life then we feel concerned about that person. A mother loves her child and if he doesn't come back from school in time then she becomes worried and starts searching for him. The mother and father of Jesus searched for him for a few days. He came with them from Galilee to celebrate the Passover festival. On the way back, they thought He was with some of the relatives in the convoy. When they realized that the child was not with them, they became worried, left everything, started searching for Him, and at last found Him in the temple. Like a mother, a wife will also become worried if she is expecting her husband to come back from his work in the evening but he doesn't come. As time passes, the level of her anxiety will keep rising. These days we have different ways of communication but in ancient times they were not able to communicate with each other instantly. In this verse, the same kind of worry is described by the bride.

The bride was waiting for the bridegroom for the whole night. Some Bible teachers say that in Hebrew the word "nights" is used instead of "night". So we see a separation between the bride and bridegroom for some considerable time. Sometimes there is a separation between us and Christ, but we hardly consider it. It happens when we are not aware of our spiritual state in Christ. Sometimes Jesus leaves us purposely to expose our intentions. Sometimes there is sin between us and Jesus. So He leaves us and doesn't answer us. In this way the main reasons that we don't find Him with us are; firstly, we don't realize that He habitually stands with us. Secondly, He leaves us to test us. Thirdly, as we keep on moving deeper and deeper into sin; then our spiritual ability to recognize His presence keeps on diminishing.

Let's look at the first reason why we don't recognize that He is with us. When God gave freedom to Israel from Egypt, they should have believed God could take care of everything. God did a great miracle when He parted the waters of the sea before Israel. God showed them that He has control over the waters. In Egypt, God changed water into blood and showed His great power. Now just three days after God showed His power over wind and water by making a way for Israelites through the sea that we see anxiety among the Israelites about drinking water. They should have realized that the God who can control the waters of rivers in Egypt and the Red Sea can provide them with an abundance of water.

Exodus 15:22-24

Moses led Israel onward from the Red Sea, and they went out into the wilderness of Shur; and they went three days in the wilderness, and found no water. When they came to Marah, they couldn't drink from the waters of Marah, for they were bitter. Therefore its name was called Marah. The people murmured against Moses, saying, "What shall we drink?"

It is not easy for anyone to go without water for days. If you go without water for three to five days then you can face serious medical problems. The Israelites were traveling for three days without water. They had little children, old people, and cattle with them. They could die without water. So they started complaining and murmuring against God and Moses. They were thinking that God brought them out of Egypt but now He has left them alone in the wilderness. They believed in God, came out of Egypt but now they were not able to find God near them. They and their loved ones might die but God wasn't visible on the scene. It looked like God had left them. In the same way, the bride was not finding the bridegroom in her room. She was worried about how she could find Him again. The difference between the Israelites and the bride was, the bride wasn't murmuring and complaining whereas the Israelites were.

God wasn't away from Israelites, but He has some rules. We need to follow those rules before He comes to help us. Ten times God sent plagues in Egypt. Every time Pharaoh called asking Moses to pray to God to remove the plague. God was able to bring a plague on the whole of Egypt and He was able to remove that through prayers. When Pharaoh came with chariots and army to kill the Israelites, it was God who kept him away from the Israelites through the prayer of Moses (Exodus 14:13-15). So the principle to see God at work on our behalf is prayer. Instead of praying, they were complaining. When we complain, we are showing that we have forgotten His past mercies and we are trying to force Him to do something for us. If we forget His previous works for us, it means we are thankless people and disregard the Lord. This is a sin; God even left His son when he was on the cross because the sin of the world was upon Him. Again, we see that the solution to the water problem didn't come through the complaints of the Israelites but through the prayers of Moses (Exodus 15:25-26).

The second reason why it seems like God has left us; when there is a test in our lives. This was the situation going on with Job. Satan wanted Job to fall in sin whereas God wanted to uplift Job's life; for this Job had to pass a test. Sometimes when we are going through tests and trials we don't see God near us, but He is always around us because He never leaves us or forsakes us.

The third reason why we don't see God near us or feel His

presence is our sin. King Saul was living his life in sin, for years. Because of his sins, an evil spirit was tormenting him. He didn't repent and ended up seeking guidance through a witch. God leaves such people and doesn't answer their prayers until they repent, but the arrogance of Saul kept him away from repentance and as a result, God left him in his sinful ways.

We don't see any sin or mistake in the bride's life to cause the bridegroom to stay away from her; therefore, this separation is not to discipline her but to test her and bless her after the test. Instead of complaining, she was searching for the bridegroom on her bed. A believer should keep on searching for God until he finds Him. The woman who was suffering from the issue of blood kept on pushing through the crowd until she reached and touched the garment of Jesus. We need to seek His presence until we find Him.

3:2

I will get up now, and go about the city; in the streets and in the squares I will seek him whom my soul loves. I sought him, but I didn't find him.

The bride talked about leaving her home and going to different places to search for the bridegroom. It is a spiritual rule that if we don't find His presence in one place, we need to change our place. His presence is our blessing, and to bless Abraham, God told him to change his place. He needed to migrate from Ur of the Chaldeans to Canaan. Rebeka needed to migrate from Paddan Aram to Canaan to take part in the blessings of Abraham. Moses saw the great visible presence of God in the bush in the wilderness, which was a blessing for him, but for further blessing, he needed to go to Egypt (Exodus Chapter 3). Throughout the journey in the wilderness, the Israelites had been following the presence of God (Numbers 9:22). They had to follow the cloud or the pillar of fire to set up their camps. They could have decided that yesterday the presence of God was at the

Red Sea and God saved us from Pharaoh there, so we should stay there and need not move. But then they would soon know that although yesterday God showed Himself at the Red Sea, today He is working at Elam. God doesn't need to follow our thoughts; we need to follow His plans. Jesus had been teaching people in one place but the next day He usually went to another place. A crowd was following Jesus, but Jesus only fed the five thousand on the third day. On the first day he shared the Word and then moved to a new place and shared the word thereon the second day. He did the same on the third day. He didn't feed them on the first or second day, He fed the people on the third day who had been following Him for all the three days (Matthew 15:32). We need to follow God. If we don't find His presence on our bed, we need to come out of that bed, which is our comfort zone. The more we follow the presence, through prayer and Word, the more we come nearer to our blessing. The more the Israelites followed the cloud, the more they were nearing their destination, Canaan. They were in the wilderness and had been getting their food, manna, under the cloud. They were getting their protection from severe heat in the day through the cloud and remained warm at night through the pillar of fire. Their lives depended on the cloud and fire which symbolized God's presence. The bride knows that she loves Jesus and can't live without Him so she was searching for His presence.

In Matthew 9:27-31, we see two blind beggars on the side of the road where Jesus was passing by. A big crowd was following Jesus. Knowing that Jesus was passing, they started calling out, *"Have mercy on us, Son of David!"* They left their clothes and followed Jesus. They could have thought that they would be hurt by going in the crowd. As the crowd was passing by, it was a good time to beg and earn money but instead of taking benefit from the situation, they started calling out to Jesus. Instead of raising their voices to collect money they raised their voices to get help from Jesus. When they tried to make their request known to Jesus, people rebuked them. Without thinking about any other thing, they started calling Jesus with a loud voice. Jesus always answers when you call Him; He never ignores you. Previously they had been begging from the passers-by. Today they were not requesting money from the crowd. They were requesting their blessing from Jesus, the blessing to see this world. In this case they were seeking Jesus. The crowd symbolizes the people or gods in which we put our trust. When we remove our attention from the crowd to Jesus, we come on the right track. From the crowd, we mean the people or gods we trust. Jesus stopped at their call for help and the whole crowd stopped with Him. The people who were rebuking them to be quiet started helping them to reach Jesus, and He healed them at that very moment. To reach Jesus, the blind men had to leave their comfort zone. They had to face opposition but, in the end, they were healed. As the bride thought of leaving her bed and going out in search of Him, we need to go out as well. She thought of searching for Him in the streets and squares. Streets are usually straight paths and squares are the places where different paths meet. It means when we go out to seek Jesus, don't only seek on the same street or path where you have been walking for years. Go to the squares as well where you will meet different people who are coming from different paths. Those believers will listen to you and help you through their own spiritual experiences. Maybe the place where we are at present is too noisy to hear His voice. Moses was alone in the wilderness when he heard God. He needed to take off his shoes to hear God's instructions. God showed him the burning bush, but to stand on the holy ground you need to remove the shoes. These shoes can be in the form of some attachments you have in your life. As the prodigal son left his friends to join his father, we need to leave the attachments which are holding us, the threads which are binding us. Matthew had to leave the post of the tax collector (Matthew 9:9). Simon and Andrew left their fishing profession to be a disciple of Christ. Are we willing to leave something which is a hindrance between us and Jesus?

3:3

The watchmen who go about the city found me; "Have you seen him whom my soul loves?"

The watchmen are the Christian leaders who stay awake and alert for the security of the church people. The people of God enjoy blessings because such leaders stand before God and intercede for the church. Psalm 134:1-3, talks about these people; "*Look! Praise Yahweh, all you servants of Yahweh, who stand by night in Yahweh's house! Lift up your hands in the sanctuary. Praise Yahweh! May Yahweh bless you from Zion, even he who made heaven and earth.*" Zion in these verses represents the church. It means the people who stand on behalf of the church for its blessing, are blessed by God. These people used to patrol around the city at night, to intercept the enemy's move against God's people.

When the bride was unable to find Christ on the bed, she contacted the watchmen of the city. This shows the necessity that we remain in contact with our leaders. It means that a church is not a one-man show. Every believer needs other believers. Every bogie (carriage) of this train needs to be attached to the other bogie. If one bogie thinks that it is self-sufficient and doesn't need anyone else, and detaches itself from the train, then that bogie will remain standing alone in some wilderness and the remaining train will continue its journey towards heaven. The church can also be seen like a giant Ferris wheel. You may have seen the giant wheel in amusement parks. Every cabin needs to be attached to the other. Every cabin must remain connected securely to the next so that the wheel retains its structure. If one cabin is detached, it will destroy itself and the people in it. Pastors need people and people need pastoral care. The pastor needs a pastoral team because he can't bear the burden alone. It is like a spiritual life cycle in which everyone needs their fellow Christians. Moses was a great leader but a time came when he admitted that he could no longer bear the burden of the nation; then God gave him seventy elders to bear the burden along with him. People were ordered to contact those seventy people if they had any problem. Moses was the type of Jesus, the savior in the Old Testament. If Moses wasn't available, those seventy elders had to lead the nation. In the New Testament, the pattern is the same. Jesus is always available to His people but now He is invisible because He is not in His bodily form. If someone has a problem in coming into His presence that person should consult the leaders in the church. The bride did the same thing, she tried at her level first but she wasn't successful, so she contacted the watchmen in the city to seek their guidance to find Christ.

David was a prophet, but he never boasted of this fact. Whenever he felt himself in trouble, he always consulted other prophets. When Saul was after David, he ran to Samuel the prophet to get guidance from the Lord. Later when he was hiding in jungles and wilderness, several times he sought help from Nathan the prophet to get guidance from the Lord. It was not only his need and practice to honor other men of God and ask them to guide him when he was running through different problems in the wilderness; he kept this practice even when he became king. No matter how low we feel within ourselves and no matter how high our status is, we should always respect the guidance from other men of God.

3:4

I had scarcely passed from them, when I found him whom my soul loves. I held him, and would not let him go, until I had brought him into my mother's house, into the room of her who conceived me.

Having Godly leaders in any church is a big blessing. The bride was worried about the separation between her and the bridegroom. According to the previous verse, she had been searching for the bridegroom at night. When she was not able to find Him, she came in contact with the watchmen, they are the leaders in the church. In this verse, she continues her speech and tells that after meeting the watchmen, she barely went a few yards away before she found the bridegroom. The good thing about her search is that she didn't stay with the watchmen. She asked them about the bridegroom and started her search again. Sometimes when we go to our spiritual leaders, we try to put the entire burden on them. We try to keep our worldly life going, but at the same time we keep on asking the pastors to keep praying for us. We like to use them as a prayer machine on which we can put all our burdens and ask that they may constantly pray for us. Sometimes we think that if we give offerings in the church and we bless the pastor, then the pastor must pray for us as we don't want to spend any time in prayer or the Word. We can't spend our spiritual life on crutches. When we depend only on the prayers of others, and we are not praying for ourselves, then it is like we are living on a ventilator or using crutches instead of our legs.

The bride only took advice from the watchmen and then started searching again. We can ask our spiritual leaders to pray for us, we can take advice but then we need to continue in our prayer life and work on the advice we get from our watchmen or spiritual leaders. It is similar to the way in which we take advice from a doctor. A doctor can give us advice but cannot take our medicine for us. We need to follow the sound advice if our leaders as we would that of a doctor. In Matthew 19:16-24, we see a conversation between a rich man and Jesus. A rich man came to get advice from Jesus. He asked, *"Good teacher, what good thing shall I do, that I may have eternal life?"* Jesus told him the answer to his problems. Jesus replied, *"If you want to be perfect, go, sell what you have, and give to the poor, and you will have treasure in heaven; and come, follow me."* This advice was not acceptable to the rich man. Like the bride, he wanted to search for God. The bride accepted the advice, whereas the rich man didn't. In 2-Kings 5, Naaman came to Israel in search of healing from Leprosy. Elisha advised him to go and wash his body seven times in the River Jordan. At first, Naaman didn't like it but later he acted upon Elisha's advice and got the healing he desired. We need to respect and give value to the advice we get from our spiritual leaders.

After finding Jesus, the bride took Him to her mother's house; the place where she was born. Her mother's house is the church where a believer is spiritually born again. When the bride was in trouble, she was searching for Christ and she got advice from the church leaders. After finding Jesus, her problem was solved. Now it was the ethical duty of the bride to say thanks to the church and church leaders who had been praying for her. She was searching for Jesus. She took Jesus with her to the church to share her testimony and to show that this is Jesus, the answer to my prayers. In the same way, when Hannah received the son for whom she had prayed, she took him to Eli and presented herself and her son before him, as he was the spiritual authority over her (1-Samuel 1:24-28). In the same way, when our problem is solved, we need to go to the church that was worried for us and prayed for us; and share the testimony. Ten lepers came to Jesus; He healed all of them. Only one of them came back to say thank you (Luke 17:11-19). Jesus wanted all of them to come back and say thanks. We also need to honor God by coming back to our mother church and show our gratitude to the church people and to God.

3:5

I adjure you, daughters of Jerusalem, by the roes, or by the hinds of the field, that you not stir up nor awaken love, until it so desires.

By reading the above verses, we know that the bride was searching for Christ. For some reason, Jesus was away from her. She knew what it looks like when Jesus is not in someone's life. When we disobey Jesus, it is a sin. Sin created a wall between God and Adam. The bride knows that doing anything against the will of Jesus gives a chance to the devil to influence our lives. To awake or disturb Jesus means doing something against His will. The bride is requesting the daughters of Jerusalem, not to disturb Him; means don't do the things which are against the will of Christ or in other words, don't fall in sin because it disturbs Jesus.

The daughters of Jerusalem are the believers in the church. Spiritually, we are growing in Christ and moving towards spiritual perfection. In this process, we sometimes fall. Mostly it is the desires of our heart or sin which causes us to fall. The bride charges the daughters of Jerusalem, or believers, by the gazelles and does. Gazelles are beautiful and expensive; only rich people could afford their meat. It was a routine dish on the table of King Solomon (1-Kings 4:23). By charging the daughters of Jerusalem, the bride was trying to show them the danger involved in going against the will of Christ. When you vow or charge someone about a particular thing or man, it means you are putting the life of that particular person in danger. Because by taking a vow you agreed to put to death that particular man if you will go against that vow. By charging the daughters of Jerusalem by the gazelles, the bride is saying that you can lose the beautiful and expensive gazelles by doing something against the will of God. God doesn't want to hurt us but Satan always seeks the opportunity to harm us. Therefore as soon as we go against the will of Jesus, we sin; the moment we sin, Satan starts working against us and tries to harm us. *The thief only comes to steal, kill, and destroy. I came that they may have life, and may have it abundantly* (John 10:10). We can learn this lesson from the life of Jacob.

Genesis 31:30-32

Now, you want to be gone, because you greatly longed for your father's house, but why have you stolen my gods?" Jacob answered Laban, "Because I was afraid, for I said, 'Lest you should take your daughters from me by force.' Anyone you find your gods with shall not live. Before our relatives, discern what is yours with me, and take it." For Jacob didn't know that Rachel had stolen them.

Genesis 35:16-18

They traveled from Bethel. There was still some distance to come to Ephrath, and Rachel travailed. She had hard labor. When she was in hard labor, the midwife said to her, "Don't be afraid, for now you will have another son." As her soul was departing (for she died), she named him Benoni, but his father named him Benjamin.

Jacob didn't know that Rachel had stolen the gods of her father. He vowed that anyone who had stolen the gods of Laban should be put to death. Unknowingly, he exposed Rachel to death. Although she escaped the wrath of her father and husband, the words of Jacob caught her. Within a few days after the vow of Jacob, Rachel died. He lost his beautiful and lovely wife. So we need to be careful about our vows. He lost the beauty of his life, his beloved wife, and his gazelle. The same fact the bride wanted us to understand. When we come to Christ, we announce that from now on, I belong to Christ. When we sin, we break our vow and Satan can take advantage of this to attack our loved ones.

3:6

Who is this who comes up from the wilderness like pillars of smoke, perfumed with myrrh and frankincense, with all spices of the merchant?

In this verse, we see someone whose appearance from far away is like a pillar of smoke and he is coming from the wilderness. Smoke doesn't have a specific shape. As smoke changes shape, God can change His appearance. So smoke in this verse represents the presence of God. To different people, God appeared differently. In Genesis 15, God appeared to Abraham as a flaming torch. In Genesis 18, Jesus appeared to Abraham as a common man. In Genesis 14:18, He appeared as Melchizedek king of Salem. In Exodus 3:2, He appeared as a small fire in a bush but in Exodus 24:17, He appeared as a consuming fire on the mountain. In Exodus 24:9-10, He appeared to seventy elders of Israelites; *Then Moses, Aaron, Nadab, Abihu, and seventy of the elders of Israel went up. They saw the God of Israel. Under his feet was like a paved work of sapphire stone, like the skies for clearness.* He appeared differently to Ezekiel, Jeremiah, and John (In the book of Revelation).

The Israelites were in the wilderness when God appeared to them in the form of consuming fire and heavy smoke. Mount Sinai was covered with smoke because the Lord descended on it in the fire. *All of Mount Sinai smoked, because Yahweh descended on it in fire; and its smoke ascended like the smoke of a furnace, and the whole mountain quaked greatly.* (Exodus 19:18). The Lord descended on Mount Sinai in the wilderness and talked with the Israelites. He told them the commandments; people accepted those commandments and entered a covenant with God. In Genesis 15:17-18, it is written, *"It came to pass that, when the sun went down, and it was dark, behold, a smoking furnace and a flaming torch passed between these pieces. In that day Yahweh made a covenant with Abram, saying,"I have given this land to your offspring, from the river of Egypt to the great river, the river Euphrates".* In both the references of Genesis 15 and Exodus 19, we see the presence of God in the form of fire and smoke. In both cases, God spoke to people and made a covenant with them. Marriage is also a covenant and God is a covenant husband of Israel. He described His covenant marriage as, *"Now when I passed by you, and looked at you, behold, your time was the time of love; and I spread my skirt over you, and covered your nakedness. Yes, I swore to you, and entered into a covenant with you," says the Lord Yahweh, "and you became mine"* (Ezekiel 16:8). As we see the pillar of smoke coming, it means God who makes covenants, is coming to meet His covenant wife.

The one who is coming is perfumed with myrrh and incense made from all the spices of the merchant. The smoke of myrrh and incense was extensively used in sacrifices in the temple. These elements represent worship. When we worship, His presence comes into our midst. He is not only perfumed with myrrh and incense but He is also perfumed with all kinds of spices of the merchant. By reading Ezekiel and Isaiah learn about this trade. *By the multitude of your iniquities, in the unrighteousness of your commerce, you have profaned your sanctuaries* (Ezekiel 28:18). *Your pomp is brought down to Sheol, with the sound of your stringed instruments* (Isaiah 14:11). These two verses talk about Satan when he was created by God. He had some musical abilities to play instruments. He was a worship leader. He used to take the worship of angels to the throne of God. This was his trade; because of this trade, he became proud and fell from his designation. When Solomon wrote that He is perfumed by myrrh and incense and all spices of the merchants; we need to remember that myrrh and incense were used by the Israelites to worship God. The spice of merchants is the worship of other nations for our God. This was a kind of trade whereby they bring their worship to God and He blessed them in all their works. The worship of God by other nations was not begun in New Testament times, even in the Old Testament we see people like Naaman who accepted God as the supreme authority in the universe and worshiped Him.

3:7

Behold, it is Solomon's carriage! Sixty mighty men are around it, of the mighty men of Israel.

Solomon is coming in His carriage. His warriors are with Him; ready to fight on behalf of Solomon. They are from the noblest of Israel. If they are from the bloodline of Israel it means they are humans, not angels. Solomon represents Jesus in Song of Songs. With God, we usually think of angelic hosts but here we see humans with the carriage. A carriage is an object on which the king used to travel. First, let's see about the carriage of God. God is all-powerful and He doesn't need any carriage or escort. The escort we see here shows the royalty, majesty, and awe due to the king. His presence is enough to protect and sustain everything. He is not only the creator of this universe; He is a King as well. Being a king, He has earthly and heavenly hosts working under His command. In Genesis 2:1 He said, "*The heavens, the earth, and all their vast array were finished*". In some translations, in place of "vast array", the word "host or hosts" is used. Heaven and earth both contain His hosts; and with His carriage on the earth, He was using earthly hosts. From earthly hosts, He chooses men of Israel, the Israelites are called the Lord's hosts in many places. In Joshua 5, we see that the commander of the army of God came to meet Joshua. That army didn't consist of angels. The army under Joshua was counted as the army or hosts of God. Joshua was ready to attack Jericho with the Israelite army and Jesus appeared to him as the commander of that human army; now it was God's army. So angels are not the only participants of the Lord's army, humans are also a part of that army.

We see the weapons of war with the host carrying the carriage. They had weapons because the enemy could attack in the dark of night. Angels and humans are both parts of the Lord's army, with Satan and his forces as their common enemy. The description of our enemy is given in Ephesians 6:12, "*For our wrestling is not against flesh and blood, but against the principalities, against the powers, against the world's rulers of the darkness of this age, and against the spiritual forces of wickedness in the heavenly place*". As our enemy is a spirit, so we need spiritual weapons to stand against him. Therefore God has given us supernatural weapons which can be seen in Ephesians 6:13-18, "*Therefore put on the whole armor of God, that you may be able to withstand in the evil day, and having done all, to stand. Stand therefore, having the utility belt of truth buckled around your waist, and having put on the breastplate of righteousness, and having fitted your feet with the preparation of the Good News of peace, above all, taking up the shield of faith, with which you will be able to quench all the fiery darts of the evil one. And take the helmet of salvation, and the sword of the Spirit, which is the word of God; with all prayer and requests, praying at all times in the Spirit, and being watchful to this end in all perseverance and requests for all the saints"* After describing the spiritual weapons, Paul advised us to pray in the Spirit. He is not asking us to pray for one hour or two, he is encouraging us to pray every time everywhere. Because, when we pray through our mind, we may need a quiet place away from the distractions of this world but when we pray in Spirit, we can pray anywhere. When we pray in Spirit then it is a conversation between our spirit and the Spirit of God (Romans 8:26). No one can distract the Spirit of God so when we grow in Christ and pray in the Spirit then distractions around us don't have much impact on us. The apostle Paul advised us to pray in both ways, through our spirit and mind (1-Corinthians 14:14-15). Paul felt it necessary to advise us about prayer after teaching us about spiritual weapons. If you have a very modern electric car, you will feel proud of it but if it doesn't have a charge in its battery, it will be of no use. Prayer is the battery for spiritual weapons. If we don't have the proper charging through prayer then spiritual weapons won't work properly. The authority Jesus has given us on demons is a weapon against Satan (Luke 10:19, Mark 16:17-18). But this weapon didn't work well when disciples were casting a demon from a boy. The father of the boy came to Jesus and complained that His disciples were not able to cast out the demon. *When he had come into the house, his disciples asked him privately, "Why couldn't we cast it out?" He said to them, "This kind can come out by nothing, except by prayer and fasting."* (Mark 9:28-29). So we see that disciples had the weapon in the form of authority over demons but it didn't work because they didn't charge their spiritual batteries with the prayer to use the weapon.

We can see sixty mighty men of Israel with Solomon's carriage. Only those people who are mighty, skilled fighters, and faithful could walk with the king's carriage. These are the people on whom the king trusts, they are ready to die for the king. They stand in the presence of the king. No one can go as near to the king as they can. Spiritually, the people who spend time in prayer and the Word of God can go near to Him, if they obey what they read from the Bible.

Enoch was one such faithful person. *Enoch walked with God, and he was not found, for God took him* (Genesis 5:24). Abraham was His friend (Isaiah 41:8). God had been talking with Moses as a friend (Exodus 33:11) David was near to the heart of God (1-Samuel 13:14). Daniel was highly esteemed (Daniel 9:23). Of people who were born through women, no one was greater than John the Baptist (Matthew 11:11). These are some of the people who had been walking with the carriage of the king, we know this because they were carrying God's presence with them and the carriage, in a way, shows His presence. God doesn't have favoritism in His presence (Romans 2:11, Galatians 2:6). If they can come near to God, we can also; but it depends on us how faithful we are to our God.

3:8

They all handle the sword, and are expert in war. Every man has his sword on his thigh, because of fear in the night.

The soldiers moving with the king are wearing their swords and they are experienced in battle. Spiritually, it is necessary for every believer to have battlefield experience. When Jesus talked about the believers, He said that their example is like a house on the rock (Matthew 7:24-25). On that house flood water had been hitting hard. These floods are the problems that come against us as a flood, where we have to stand firm and fight against the spiritual forces. The Israelites who came out of Egypt were not able to go into Canaan because they were afraid of fighting. It looks like the Israelite men were fighting against the people of Canaan but behind the scene, there was a big spiritual battle going on. In Joshua 5:13-14, we see Jesus as the commander of the Lord's army because, alongside the Israelites, angels fought for God's people. In 2-Kings 19:35, we see that the Lord sent an angel and he killed one hundred and eighty-five thousand people from the army which came against Israel. In spiritual battles, we don't kill anyone. We see swords with the soldiers but Ephesians 6:17 teaches us that the sword of the spirit is the Word of God. Through the sword of the Word, we see things happen in the natural and supernatural world. The creation of the whole world is by the word spoken by God. We see the people being healed by the word spoken by Jesus and His disciples in the four gospels and the Acts of the Apostles. When God created the world, everything was perfect and good. *God saw everything that he had made, and, behold, it was very good. There was evening and there was morning, a sixth day* (Genesis 1:31). Satan brought destruction, disease, and death through sin. In John 5, Jesus healed a man who had been an invalid for thirty-eight years. Jesus released the Word by saying, *"Arise, take up your mat, and walk." Immediately, the man was made well, and took up his mat and walked* (John 5:8-9). Along with the healing, Jesus gave him specific instructions. He said, *"Behold, you are made well. Sin no more, so that nothing worse happens to you"* (John 5:14). In Genesis 1, we see that God created everything by His Word. In Genesis 3, Satan sows the imperfect seeds of sin, which resulted in physical and spiritual sickness. In John 5, we see that Jesus removed the sickness by His Word. So the word has the creative power, and if anything goes wrong with the creation it has healing power as well. By giving authority over demons, sickness, and the works of the enemy (Mark 16:17-18, John 14:13-14), He has given the same power in the Word which will be released from our mouth in the name of Jesus (Acts 3:6).

The swords on the thighs of the soldiers show the readiness of the soldiers to use it as soon as they feel some danger. They were traveling with the king at night. The night in the Word represents sinful acts of the dark world. *The night is far gone, and the day is near. Let's therefore throw off the deeds of darkness, and let's put on the armor of light* (Romans 13:12). All the people who have accepted Christ are "light" and sons or daughters of light (Matthew 5:14, Luke 16:8, John 12:36). If anybody from the world of darkness attacks us we need to be ready to use the sword of the Spirit and respond properly. When Jesus was telling His disciples that He would be crucified,

Satan attacked Jesus through Peter. Peter didn't realize that Satan was using him. Jesus immediately responds and said, *"Get behind me, Satan! You are a stumbling block to me, for you are not setting your mind on the things of God, but on the things of men"* (Matthew 16:23). When Jesus was in the wilderness and Satan came to tempt Him, He used scriptures to answer him. Jesus used the sword of the Spirit to defeat him.

3:9

King Solomon made himself a carriage of the wood of Lebanon.

Lebanon is well known in present days, and also in ancient days, for its wood. Solomon got wood for his house and temple from Lebanon. The carriage of King Solomon was made of wood from Lebanon. The carriage is the carrier that takes Solomon from one place to another and it is made by Solomon. Solomon was the King over Israel for a short period, but God is the king over Israel till eternity. We need to see what His carriage looks like. Clouds and air work as His carriage. *He rode on a cherub, and flew. Yes, he soared on the wings of the wind* (Psalm 18:10). *He makes the clouds his chariot. He walks on the wings of the wind* (Psalm 104:3). Angels are mightier than humans, and among the angels, cherubim are considered the most powerful angels. Accordingly, we can say that after God, cherubim are the most powerful creatures in the universe. When God uses them as His chariot, it shows the power and glory of God to keep everything under His control. Sometimes we are afraid of the powerful rulers of this earth or officers that are against us, but we need to remember that if He could create and control the most powerful beings in the universe then He can control every other person as well.

In Ezekiel 1 and 10, we read the description of the throne of God above the cherubim. *Above the expanse that was over their heads was the likeness of a throne, as the appearance of a sapphire stone. On the likeness of the throne was a likeness as the appearance of a man on it above* (Ezekiel 1:26). *Then I looked, and see, in the expanse that was over the head of the cherubim there appeared above them as it were a sapphire stone, as the appearance of the likeness of a throne* (Ezekiel 10:1). The same kind of throne was seen by the seventy elders of Israel. *Then Moses, Aaron, Nadab, Abihu, and seventy of the elders of Israel went up. They saw the God of Israel. Under his feet was like a paved work of sapphire stone, like the skies for clearness* (Exodus 24:9-10). We see at least three times that when God appeared to His people on a throne, its appearance was like a blue-colored stone. As God used cherubim, the best in the universe to lay His throne over them, Solomon made his carriage with the best available wood from Lebanon. When we take it spiritually, God made His throne above the cherubim (the most powerful creatures) with a blue-colored stone. But God doesn't need a throne made by physical stone. He is a spirit and He doesn't need a physical throne. By showing His throne at different times and His glory in Ezekiel Chapter 1 and Revelation Chapter 1, He wanted to tell us that He is almighty and we need to respect Him more than all the kings and kingdoms of this universe.

A throne and a footstool go along with each other. Earth is the footstool of the Lord. This is what the Lord says: *Heaven is my throne, and the earth is my footstool. What kind of house will you build to me? Where will I rest?* (Isaiah 66:1)

Nothing is as vast and beautiful as the whole heaven. So we can't make anything better for Him, but in His love, He accepts everything which we bring in His presence. Showing heaven as His throne, God is saying that He is mightier than our thoughts. Heaven doesn't have any limits. Scientists are unable to find the length and depth of heaven. The more they explore, the more depth they find. So God's throne or kingdom is infinite. We know that a footstool is always smaller than the throne; the earth is the footstool of God which is smaller than heaven. In reality, God doesn't need a footstool. Earth being His footstool means God has complete authority over the earth and nothing is hidden from Him. He knows everything, and His presence is everywhere.

3:10

He made its pillars of silver, its bottom of gold, its seat of purple, the middle of it being paved with love, from the daughters of Jerusalem.

Posts and bases are very important parts of the carriage. Posts help in movement and without a base, no one can sit in the carriage. Posts are made of silver. Silver represents salvation in the Bible. It means God's carriage or His presence moves because he wants the salvation of mankind. He is a loving God who doesn't want anyone to perish. So our salvation is the driving force behind the move of God. Salvation doesn't only mean deliverance from sins. It is an ongoing process that involves almost all aspects of our lives. Healing of sick bodies, growing in revelations of Christ, and leaving the bad habits or company is also included in our salvation. The process of salvation never ends during our lifetime. When we die, we are delivered from the worries and troubles of this life; this is another kind of salvation. *For we know that if the earthly house of our tent is dissolved, we have a building from God, a house not made with hands, eternal, in the heavens. For most certainly in this we groan, longing to be clothed with our habitation which is from heaven, if indeed being clothed, we will not be found naked. For indeed we who are in this tent do groan, being burdened, not that we desire to be unclothed, but that we desire to be clothed, that what is mortal may be swallowed up by life* (2-Corinthians 5:1-4).

Without the base, nothing can be erected inside the carriage. The carriage can't go anywhere without its posts. Silver and gold are parts of the carriage which means the presence of God and salvation goes together. The psalmist admits this fact and says, "When my enemies turn back, they stumble and perish in your presence" (Psalm

9:3). The enemy doesn't only mean people who are against us; it also means sickness, the work of Satan in our family or workplace, accidents, etc. The enemy doesn't only attack once, he comes again and again, but every time the presence of God is enough to protect us. Balak and Balaam tried to curse Israel again and again, but the presence of God always protected the Israelites (Numbers chapter 21-23). Gold as a base of the carriage means God himself upholds everything for our salvation. Salvation is His plan and He provides everything to accomplish it. In the previous verse, we read that Solomon got the wood from Lebanon to make the carriage. From the Bible, we know that Solomon was a big fan of cedars from Lebanon. Cedar is the wood which repels snakes. Sometimes people put cedar shavings around their houses to keep snakes away. In the Bible wood represents humans. Jesus was the human on whom Satan was not able to crawl or defeat. He was the human from whom demons used to flee away, as snakes stay away from cedar wood. Now if we combine the wood, silver, and gold of the carriage, we can see the plan of salvation in the imagery of the carriage; that God will come in the form of a human who will bring salvation to this world.

The cushion or the covering of the seat was purple. Usually, kings used purple-colored. The cushion with purple color means this was the seat of the king. No one else was allowed to sit there. No one can take Jesus' place because no one is as holy as Jesus. No one can say like Jesus said, "*Which of you convicts me of sin?*" None of the other prophets raised the dead and healed the sick as Jesus did. No one is able to finish the process of Salvation, except Jesus (John 19:30). So no one else can take His place because He is the King of Kings and the Lord of Lords (Revelation 19:16).

The daughters of Jerusalem worked on the interior of the carriage with love. Love is the base of all the things God does for us and he wants the same kind of love from us. He is not after precious gifts from us. He only wants our undivided love and attention. Jesus appreciated the small giving of a widow instead of the big offerings of other people. When a room is being prepared for a king, everything there should be arranged according to the king's taste. As our king is inspired by the love we have for Him, therefore the interior of the carriage should be maintained with love. It means we need to prepare the king's carriage with love, so that His presence may come and stay among us. Love is the desired interior Jesus wants for His carriage. Angels or any creation other than humans can't provide love. This is why daughters of Jerusalem (meaning believers), are the only ones who can prepare the interior of the carriage. His presence doesn't come in our midst if He doesn't see love in us. If He sees love in us then we become His carriage to take Him to the world which is suffering from sickness and diseases. When people worship God he comes in their midst. So worship attracts God to move among us and worshipers are the carriage of God. We have already seen that this whole carriage shows the plan of salvation for humanity. If we are worried about the salvation of our loved ones then our love for our people and our love for Christ becomes the driving force for Christ to act on our behalf and save our loved ones. It was out of the love the disciples had for the salvation of the world that almost all the disciples died as martyrs. Our salvation is not cheap. The blood of Christ, His followers, and the prayers of righteous people are the basis of the salvation which we are enjoying without paying any cost.

3:11

Go out, you daughters of Zion, and see king Solomon, with the crown with which his mother has crowned him, in the day of his weddings, in the day of the gladness of his heart.

Zion is the name of a hill in Jerusalem. There was a fort of Jebusites on the top of the hill named Zion, which was conquered by David (2-Samuel 5:7). When that city was captured, it was named, "The City of David". In the last verse, we read about the Daughters of Jerusalem but here we read about Daughters of Zion. Most of the Bible teachers say that there is no difference between daughters of Jerusalem and daughters of Zion because Zion is the part of Jerusalem. But I feel there is a difference between them. Zion was a part of Jerusalem, similarly Jews who believed Jesus were in small numbers, but they were part of a wider Jewish community. So the daughters of Jerusalem represent Old Testament believers or a bigger community of Jews and the daughters of Zion represent New Testament believers. We can see this in the book of Revelation also. *I heard the number of those who were sealed, one hundred forty-four thousand, sealed out of every tribe of the children of Israel* (Revelation 7:4). *I saw, and behold, the Lamb standing on Mount Zion, and with him a number, one hundred forty-four thousand, having his name, and the name of his Father, written on their foreheads. I heard a sound from heaven, like the sound of many waters, and like the sound of a great thunder. The sound which I heard was like that of harpists playing on their harps. They sing a new song before the throne, and before the four living creatures and the elders. No one could learn the song except the one hundred forty-four thousand, those who had been redeemed out of the earth* (Revelation 14:1-3). We see that these are the people from the tribes of Israel. But, at the same time, they are believers under the New Testament standing on Mount Zion. Through Jesus' sacrifice, an era of the New Testament started. Isaiah 4:4-5, 2:3, Hebrews 12:22, and 1-Peter 2:5-7 are the prophecies that are fulfilled in the New Testament. In these prophecies, God used the word "Zion" to indicate the New Testament believers. So again we see that so daughters of Zion represent New Testament believers.

The daughters of Zion are asked to come and look at the king who is wearing a crown and He is coming to take His wife home. When Jesus comes again, He will come in the glory of the Father with His angels (Matthew 16:27). This will be a day of immense joy for the bride (church) and bridegroom (Jesus). The bridegroom is crowned by His mother. This verse is certainly not talking about mother Mary. Mother Mary died, and Jesus never married in His earthly life. After her death, we don't see many references about her but the church, on the whole, is known as the mother of believers

(Galatians 4:26). In His earthly life, Jesus called the believers His close relatives like mother and brothers (Luke 8:19-21). To crown, someone doesn't always mean to put a crown on someone's head. It also has a symbolic meaning of giving praise and showing appreciation (Philippians 4:1, 1-Thessalonians 2:19, Hebrews 2:9). So by saying that His mother crowned Him on the day of His wedding, it simply means believers will present Him joy, praise, and worship on the day when He will come to take us home.

4:1

Behold, you are beautiful, my love. Behold, you are beautiful. Your eyes are like doves behind your veil. Your hair is as a flock of goats, that descend from Mount Gilead.

The bridegroom is fascinated by the beauty of the bride. Twice He said that she was beautiful. This repetition shows that the emphasis of Solomon in this verse is about the beauty of the bride. In Song of Songs 1:5-6, the bride said, *"I am dark, but lovely, you daughters of Jerusalem, like Kedar's tents, like Solomon's curtains. Don't stare at me because I am dark"*. This means she doesn't have the beauty of her own, and Christ is not talking about her physical beauty. Although He is pointing out her outward appearance but He is referring to her inward beauty. Jesus was never fascinated by someone's color or features. He can look inside us, and He treats people according to their inner self. Pharisees and the teachers of the law usually had an impressive outward appearance. They used to dress up nicely and were considered well respected among the people, but Jesus was not impressed by them. He said, *"Woe to you, scribes and Pharisees, hypocrites! For you are like whitened tombs, which outwardly appear beautiful, but inwardly are full of dead men's bones and of all uncleanness. Even so you also outwardly appear righteous to men, but inwardly you are full of hypocrisy and iniquity"* (Matthew 23:27-28).

People used to think good about Pharisees because of their religious outlook but there are other people as well who don't appear religious, but they are considered well in the sight of God, whereas people thought evil about them. For example, we read about a centurion in New Testament. Jesus was requested to heal the servant of a centurion. A centurion had to work in the Roman army. Romans were the oppressors of Israel. So generally Jews hated such people. Jesus could have said that he didn't want to help such a man. Jesus accepted his request to heal his servant and wanted to go to his house but the centurion sent a message to Jesus, *"Jesus went with them. When he was now not far from the house, the centurion sent friends to him, saying to him, "Lord, don't trouble yourself, for I am not worthy for you to come under my roof. Therefore I didn't even think myself worthy to come to you; but say the word, and my servant will be healed"* (Luke 7:6-7). The centurion's words revealed his faith. When Jesus heard this, he was amazed at him, and turning to the crowd following him, he said, *"I tell you, I have not found such great faith, no, not in Israel"* (Luke 7:9). So Jesus didn't like Pharisees because they were not beautiful inwardly but He praised the centurion because of his inner beauty. Similarly, Jesus calls His bride beautiful no matter what the world says about her. He likes her inner beauty.

Jesus praised the eyes of the bride. Eyes are the organ that is used to see the world. So Jesus appreciated His bride, the way she looks at the world. Her eyes were behind the veil. In eastern countries, some women use the Abaya. Abaya has a veil for the face of women. Women can see through the veil but other people can't see the face or eyes behind the veil. In Genesis 24:65, we see that when Rebecca saw Isaac for the first time before the marriage, she covered herself with a veil. In Song of Songs Chapter 8, Jesus the king came to take his wife for the wedding but in chapter 4, the bride is not yet married to the bridegroom, so she is using a veil to cover herself. Jesus said that the eyes of His bride are like doves. Doves were used as a sacrifice in the Old Testament. By the blood of sacrifice, the sins were covered and it opened a way of reconciliation between God and man. It means when the bride looks at the world, she thinks of the atonement and bringing the world to Christ.

The bridegroom compared the hair of the bride with a flock of goats descending from the hills of Gilead. Black goats descending from a hill look like a woman with wavy hair. The bridegroom compared the hair of the bride with a flock of goats descending from the hills of Gilead. Sometimes people look at the hair and by the health of hair, they can infer how healthy and strong the person is because according to some beauticians, the condition of hair indicates the inner health of a person. Spiritually we can say that the health of the bride's hair indicates the strong spiritual health of the bride. As hair is given for the covering, it means the bride has a strong spiritual covering that is Christ himself. Black goats descending from a hill look like a woman with wavy hair. Apostle Paul said, *"But if a woman has long hair, it is a glory to her, for her hair is given to her for a covering"* (1-Corinthians 11:15). So by talking about the hair of the bride, He is saying that His bride has a respectable personality. It is good if the husband and wife may respect each other, not only for the outward beauty but for the inward beauty they have. We need to request God to open our eyes to see the inward beauty of our partner otherwise we will only focus on the bad things. Outward beauty fascinates for a short while but inward beauty is long-lasting. As Jesus gives respect to the bride (His church), we should also be respectful towards the church. Some people speak against the church without thinking but we should keep in mind that if we speak against the church, we will be speaking against Jesus Christ. When Paul was persecuting the church, Jesus appeared to him and said, *"He fell on the earth, and heard a voice saying to him, "Saul, Saul, why do you persecute me?" He said, "Who are you, Lord?" The Lord said, "I am Jesus, whom you are persecuting. But rise up and enter into the city, then you will be told what you must do"* (Acts 9:4-5). If anyone comes against the church, he will be standing against Christ. So we need to respect the church.

4:2

Your teeth are like a newly shorn flock, which have come up from the washing, where every one of them has twins. None is bereaved among them.

The bridegroom is comparing the teeth of the bride with sheep. Normally sheep are white, and healthy clean teeth are also white. A healthy sheep will lay healthy lambs. If she is laying twins, it means she is quite strong that can carry two lambs in her womb and she is healthy enough to feed two lambs along with herself. The sheep which give good wool is a valuable asset. The bride's teeth are like a flock of sheep, newly shorn. These sheep are washed after being shorn. It means now they don't have any extra or dirty hair on their body. This shows that the bride's teeth are properly clean, they are healthy, and don't have any extra growth.

Teeth support the structure of the face which is the main part of our physical appearance. If the teeth are broken, the face will lose its firmness and smoothness. If teeth are not healthy, there will be pain and swelling which could be seen from the outside as well. The bridegroom is saying that the beauty of your face is because of the strong teeth you have. So Jesus is saying that your outward beauty is supported by the inward beauty you have. Inwardly your strong structure is evidenced by the smoothness of your face.

Teeth are an important part of our body. They help in chewing the food to satisfy our appetite and keep our bodies healthy. Without food, we can't survive and teeth make the food digestible by chewing it. Spiritually, the food for the whole body of Christ is the Word of God. We need to chew the food of the Word and the teachings shared from the platform of the church. If we properly chew the food, it will digest properly and transfer energy to every part of the body. This chewing of the Word is the key to success in our life. All of us want to be successful in our lives. Joshua was given the formula to walk on the path of success which says, *"This book of the law shall not depart from your mouth, but you shall meditate on it day and night, that you may observe to do according to all that is written in it; for then you shall make your way prosperous, and then you shall have good success"* (Joshua 1:8). Meditation on the Law of God is the key to success. The word "meditation" used in this verse has a deep profound meaning. In Hebrew it means, to moan, growl, utter, speak, and muse. So the meaning of meditation is to keep on thinking about the Word, learn it, use it in different situations, speak it, and talk about it with others. We need to chew the Word as we chew chewing gum, as sheep chew the cud. A sheep or cow brings the cud again and again under her teeth to chew it; we need to bring the Word again and again to our mind to keep on thinking about it. When we do this, our focus will remain on God and people will see its reflection in our works. God will see it and bless us in everything we will do.

Teeth represent two things for the church, first the spiritual food we are taking in and second the structure of the face or our appearance to the world. In the Bible two kinds of spiritual food are discussed; solid food and milk. *As newborn babies, long for the pure milk of the Word, that with it you may grow* (1-Peter 2:2). *For although by this time you should be teachers, you again need to have someone teach you the rudiments of the first principles of the revelations of God. You have come to need milk, and not solid food. For everyone who lives on milk is not experienced in the word of righteousness, for he is a baby. But solid food is for those who are full grown, who by reason of use have their senses exercised to discern good and evil* (Hebrews 5:12-14). We need both kinds of food. They will help us in our spiritual growth. This growth will make us strong inwardly and its effects will be seen outwardly. Our spiritual teeth play an important role in this whole process. The more we grow spiritually, the stronger our teeth will be. As a child grows up, he sheds his milk teeth and becomes able to chew harder things with his new, strong teeth. Our spiritual growth has nothing to do with our physical growth. An old man can be a spiritual baby and a teenager can behave like a spiritual adult. We need strong spiritual teeth to chew the hard spiritual facts. We can have such teeth at any age by asking God to help us in our spiritual growth. This spiritual growth and strong teeth will contribute to the beauty of our spiritual face and appearance.

4:3

Your lips are like scarlet thread. Your mouth is lovely. Your temples are like a piece of a pomegranate behind your veil.

Lips and mouth are associated with speech. Jesus is appreciating the speech of the bride in this verse. Her speech contains a warning for non-believers and appreciation for believers. She warns with love the many who are going on the path of death. She wants to bring them back to the way of life. The words can heal the wounds in someone's spirit. That's why God commanded Isaiah to speak loudly to the Israelites. *"Cry aloud! Don't spare! Lift up your voice like a trumpet! Declare to my people their disobedience, and to the house of Jacob their sins"* (Isaiah 58:1). God wasn't asking Isaiah to shout out the sins of the Israelites to them because He likes some kind of blame game. He is doing this because He knows if He will not warn them, they can die in their sins. Sin causes spiritual diseases like envy, wrath, lust, greed, etc. When you go to a good doctor, he doesn't only tell you about your disease, he will also tell you the cause of disease. Similarly, God saw the deadly spiritual diseases in the Israelites; He wanted to heal His people, but He needed to explain the cause of the disease, so that His people may remain safe in the future. If someone is suffering from liver disease, the doctor may advise him to avoid alcohol which is a cause of this disease. Similarly, the bride has to tell the world about their sins and God's redeeming power to save them. It is the mouth of the bride which utters words to save the world.

The mouth of the bride is the mouthpiece of God. God speaks to His people and the world through His bride. Her lips are scarlet.

Scarlet was considered as the royal color. *Then the governor's soldiers took Jesus into the Praetorium, and gathered the whole garrison together against him. They stripped him and put a scarlet robe on him* (Matthew 27:27-28). Soldiers put a scarlet robe on Jesus to ridicule Him as a king. The scarlet color was also used in the curtains of the tabernacle and the dress of high priest. Scarlet is related to the blood of Christ which brings purity and righteousness. Some people relate scarlet with sin; *"Though your sins are as scarlet, they shall be as white as snow"* (Isaiah 1:18). By combining these facts, we come to the point that Jesus is the king who purges sin and brings righteousness in the lives. Comparing the bride's lips with scarlet ribbons means the words which come out of the bride's mouth, are about the king and His kingdom. The words of praise and worship also come by her lips. Jesus Christ, John the Baptist, and Jesus' disciples all preached about the kingdom of God. This is the topic that we see from the first book of the New Testament until the last book. This kingdom starts in our lives and remains continuous even after our physical death. When we die, we die to this world. We remain alive to God, so after death, we go to heaven and remain there with Christ in His kingdom. We will be singing songs of our king there. Therefore the lips which worship God are precious and beautiful like a scarlet ribbon.

The bride's temples are likened to the halves of a pomegranate. Pomegranate has a hard cover to protect the seeds inside. They all are connected. The Word of God which the bride has inside her needs to be protected strongly otherwise Satan can snatch it. All verses in the Bible are connected to each other. This is why Bible verses explain each other. Pomegranate is an important fruit which we can see at different places in the Bible, like Exodus 28:33, 1-Kings 7:20, 2-Kings 25:17, 2-Chronicles 3:16, 4:13. There is one common thing about these references; we see the pomegranates attached to some chain where they are repeated one after another. We see them in the dress of the high priest. *On its hem you shall make pomegranates of blue, and of purple, and of scarlet, all around its hem; with bells of gold between and around them* (Exodus 28:33). These pomegranates represent fruits of the Spirit and bells represent gifts of the Spirit. Bells make a sound but pomegranates don't. Spiritual gifts like prophecy, words of knowledge, and words of wisdom are vocal gifts, so the sound is there when they are being used. But the fruits of the Spirit are hidden in your spirit. They don't make a sound but they are visible in our actions; we can feel their taste. By comparing the temples of the bride with pomegranates, it means the thoughts of the bride are centered on spiritual things. We need to know the center of our thoughts because the way we think, represents the kind of person we are. That is why the psalmist says, *"Let the words of my mouth and the meditation of my heart be acceptable in your sight, Yahweh, my rock, and my redeemer"* (Psalm 19:14). These thoughts are linked together with the Word of God as pomegranates are seen linked with each other in the Bible.

4:4

Your neck is like David's tower built for an armory, on which a thousand shields hang, all the shields of the mighty men.

The tower of David is a historical place. It is situated in Jerusalem near the Jaffa gate. This tower bore many attacks throughout history. Byzantine Christians believed that this place was the palace of King David. These days it is used as a museum and it shows the history of Jerusalem from the early days till now.

A tower is a strong high structure wherefrom its height the enemy could be spotted far off, and it ensures the safety of the city from sudden attack. If an enemy is spotted, immediately a message is sent to the inhabitants of the city to get ready for war. The neck of the bride is a tower to protect the citizens of the heavenly kingdom. The tower was usually built with stones and used as an armory. Warriors used to hang their shields in the armory to use them as soon as it was needed to protect the city. Now the neck of the bride is like a strong tower which protects the people and arms them according to their need. God speaks to the world through His bride. Jesus said, *"Go and make disciples of all nations, baptizing them in the name of the Father and of the Son and of the Holy Spirit, teaching them to observe all things that I commanded you. Behold, I am with you always, even to the end of the age." Amen* (Matthew 28:19-20). By giving the command to go to different nations and teach them the Word, Jesus was asking us to use ourselves as a tower; to inform the world about the upcoming Day of Judgment, and the salvation, love, and sacrifice of Christ. The Church has to use the teachings given by Jesus to save the world. The church is made by God, who made it using the scriptures as building blocks and the sacrifice of Jesus as the material to cement those blocks together. Normal building blocks or rocks show the effects of wear and tear which comes over time, but the building blocks of scripture have never altered their shape, effectiveness, or strength for hundreds of years. The speech of the church is a tower and scriptures are the armories to equip the believers.

Jesus doesn't only use His bride to tell people about sin and salvation, He also informs people about the good and bad which can come to this world. God used His people to inform the world about the exact time of Christ's birth and death (Daniel 9:20-27). In Daniel 8:5-8, 21-22 we get the prophecy about Alexander the Great. It is mentioned even before his birth that he will conquer the Medes and Persians. Whatever God spoke through His bride, proved correct. God also told us about the upcoming events in the book of Revelation. Nobody can alter what He has already said. His bride uses her neck to tell the people to come to Him.

4:5

Your two breasts are like two fawns that are twins of a roe, which feed among the lilies.

Christ compares the breasts of the bride with two fawns of a gazelle. The gazelle is a wild animal. Their kids are very active and hardly stay still. They always want to run around and come again and again to get a feed from their mother. Breasts are the means to feed others. As fawns are getting their feed properly in a good place where lilies are, they will grow in a better way. The Word of God is always the source of food for the believers. We have two sources of the Word of God. One is the Bible and the second is the revelations we get from God. Revelations are the key element in Christian teaching. They are the two breasts of the bride through which she feeds spiritual food to the young in the church. Without revelations, we will have only the knowledge of the Bible. Anyone can have that knowledge by reading the Bible, whether he is a believer or not. Many people who speak against God read the Bible to find something to create confusion and distract people. They know the Word but don't have the revelation of the Word. Many people act in the same way. They read the Bible and go to church just to perform a religious activity. They don't have a deeper relationship with Christ, and revelations come from the relationship with Christ. Revelations make the Bible alive. They help in our growth in Christianity. On the other hand, we need to be very careful about the revelations. The knowledge we get through revelations shouldn't be against the written Word of God. Revelations and the written Word should go side by side, supporting each other. If our spiritual knowledge and relationship are growing in Christ through Revelations and the written Word, then they will act like twin fawns that are growing together.

All the letters written in the New Testament by Paul and the disciples of Christ are the revelations they got from Christ and they have their basis in the Old Testament, the written Word of God. The whole Bible is the Word of God and all the new revelations must be based on the old revelations given by God in the Bible. All the heresies in the world are there because that knowledge is not based on the truths of the Bible. In Matthew 16:6, 12 Jesus talked with His disciples, *"Take heed and beware of the yeast of the Pharisees and Sadducees" Then they understood that he didn't tell them to beware of the yeast of bread, but of the teaching of the Pharisees and Sadducees.* Jesus warned His disciples to be careful of the words of the Pharisees and Sadducees because they were teaching the Word mixing with their traditions. A time came when they were giving more value to their traditions than the Word of God. Slowly they were going away from the Word, so Jesus had to say, *"You are therefore badly mistaken"* (Mark 12:27). Jesus has given the duty to the church to feed the believers. But the church can't feed others until they first get their food from Christ. The word "El-Shaddai" is the name of God (Genesis 28:23, 35:11, 49:25). It appeared twelve times in the Bible. It is translated as "God Almighty" or "My Supplier". But Shaddai means, breasts. So El-Shaddai means, God who has breasts. This word teaches us that our God feeds us like a mother feeds her child. Like a mother, He is our supplier. He does everything for us, He is our God Almighty. The church needs to spend time in His presence to suck the milk of Word; only then the church will be able to feed the nation. Isaiah 66:11 says, *"Rejoice with Jerusalem, and be glad for her, all you who love her. Rejoice for joy with her, all you who mourn over her; that you may nurse and be satisfied at the comforting breasts; that you may drink deeply, and be delighted with the abundance of her glory."*

As Jerusalem represents church, so people who love the church are mourned because they have seen the destruction Satan has done in the church, they are the people who intercede for the church. They are the people who will be comforted and be fed by the comforting breasts of the church as the mother of believers when God revives His church.

4:6

Until the day is cool, and the shadows flee away, I will go to the mountain of myrrh, to the hill of frankincense.

This is a kind of prophetic verse that told the Israelites about the lifestyle of Jesus Christ. Jesus used to spend a lot of time in prayer. Sometimes He spent the whole night in prayer, on other occasions we see Him rising early to spend enough time in prayer before starting a day. "Until the day is cool, and the shadows flee away" show the time of the early morning. Solomon wrote that before starting the day Jesus will go to the mountain of myrrh and the hill of incense. Myrrh and incense are related to the priestly ministry, but they also represent worship and prayer. It was the duty of the high priest to burn incense every day in the morning before the Lord in the tabernacle (Exodus 30:7) and to worship God. The incense was made by mixing different ingredients. Myrrh on the other hand was an ingredient of anointing oil. Myrrh was presented to Jesus as a sign of worship (Matthew 2:11). It was also used for the cleansing and beauty treatment of the brides (Esther 2:12).

God visited Adam and Eve in the cool of the day (Genesis 3:8). The cool of the day could mean evening or morning time but some people believe it was the morning time because that time is the coolest part of the day. Jesus also kept the early morning as His time to meet God. Jesus let us know where to find him in this verse; if you want to meet or find Him, go to the mountain of myrrh and incense. It was the duty of the priest to burn them in the morning and lay a sacrifice on the altar. According to the Apostle Peter, we are the priests of the present day. When we leave our beds early in the morning to stay in His presence, it is our sacrifice. These days we don't burn myrrh or incense but our praise and worship work as myrrh and incense. The mountain of myrrh and incense is not a specific physical place, but this mountain can be built in every house. It is not a physical mountain. It is a mountain of praise and worship. So you can meet Him right in your living room. He wants to visit every one of us. If you build an altar of worship for Him, He will build a safe spiritual environment around you. When you start worshiping the Lord, the Lord will expect you to take off your sandals. These sandals represent different shortcomings in our lives like lies, backbiting, stealing, or any other thing which can be a hindrance between us and Jesus. When we remove such things from our lives, we may receive heavy anointing in our lives. If we have difficulty leaving any habit then we can ask Jesus and He will help us. *When the Lord shall have washed away the filth of the daughters of Zion, and shall have purged the blood of Jerusalem from within it, by the spirit of justice and by the spirit of burning. Yahweh will create over the whole habitation of Mount Zion and over her assemblies, a cloud and smoke by day, and the shining of a flaming fire by night, for over all the glory will be a canopy* (Isaiah 4:4-6).

When Jacob was fleeing from His brother, he worshiped God on a mountain (Genesis 28:10-18). That mountain became the mountain of myrrh and the hill of incense where Jacob met God. The lady who poured perfume on the feet of Jesus and washed His feet with her tears, was standing in the house of a Pharisee (Luke 7:36-48). That house became the mountain of myrrh for her. But, the Pharisee who was sitting in the same house remained untouched by the blessing the woman received. Sometimes people remain frustrated and say, "I am the only believer in the house; it is difficult for me to worship God". I think it was even more difficult for the woman who worshiped Jesus in the house of the Pharisee. She was considered as the worst of sinners by the house owner. At the same time, she was scolded harshly by the disciples of Christ. She was humiliated in front of her city people, religious leaders, and family members, as her brother and sister were also present there (John 11:1-2, 12:1-6); but Jesus considered her the best person in that house. It doesn't matter what the people or our family members think about us, if you meet Him on the mountain of myrrh and hill of incense with the heart full of worship, He will convert your enemies into your friends (Proverbs 16:7).

4:7

You are all beautiful, my love. There is no spot in you.

In the previous verses of this chapter, we saw that the bridegroom was praising the lips, neck, and teeth of the bride. Now He is saying that not only the face or neck is exceptional, but she is altogether beautiful. Jesus doesn't see any flaw in His bride. We are the bride of Christ in individual and group format as the church. The people who came out from Egypt were from one nation who knew God for hundreds of years; even then they were not perfect. They had been sinning against God. God called Israel His wife (Ezekiel 16:8-21). We can see the shortcomings in Israel at any time of history; then how can God say that His wife or His people are flawless?

The Day of Atonement was important in the life of every Israelite because on that day an atonement was made for the whole nation and their sins were forgiven (Leviticus 23:27). The blood of the lamb covered their sins. It was not because of their good works or righteousness; it was by the mercy and love of God. A lamb was slain to cover their sins. The death which should be borne by Israelite was borne by the lamb. That lamb bore the sins of the Israelites, but Jesus bore the sins of the whole world. By covering the sins of the Israelites, God made Israel (His wife), flawless. Jesus died for the world; He shed His blood to forgive the sins of the world. He took the people who believed in Him and called them a church and took the church as His wife (Revelation 21:9). The blood of lambs and bulls only covered the sins (Romans 4:7) but the blood of Jesus Christ removed the sins (Romans 11:27, Hebrews 1:3).

When Jesus says that His wife is flawless, it doesn't mean that he is talking about the physical features of a particular person. Apostle Paul was a member of the church but he had some kind of physical illness. Paul wrote, *"By reason of the exceeding greatness of the revelations, that I should not be exalted excessively, a thorn in the flesh was given to me: a messenger of Satan to torment me, that I should not be exalted excessively. Concerning this thing, I begged the Lord three times that it might depart from me. He has said to me, "My grace is sufficient for you, for my power is made perfect in weakness." Most gladly therefore I will rather glory in my weaknesses, that the power of Christ may rest on me"* (2-Corinthians 12:7-9). Most Bible teachers believe that the thorn he is talking about is some kind of physical problem in his body. Similarly, we see that the eyes of Isaac and Jacob were not working properly in their old age (Genesis 27:1, 48:10). So we see physical problems or flaws in the bodies of the Old and New Testament believers; then how does Jesus is saying that His bride is flawless? The bride or the church is flawless not because of its beauty or health. His bride is flawless because of the work done by Jesus on the cross for the salvation of the world.

Now whoever believes in Him becomes the partaker of the flawless work of Christ. We get the righteousness of Christ; this unmatchable righteousness makes us flawless. Our righteousness is not enough to take us into the presence of God. So we depend on the flawless righteousness given by Christ. *But now apart from the law, a righteousness of God has been revealed, being testified by the law and the prophets; even the righteousness of God through faith in Jesus Christ to all and on all those who believe. For there is no distinction, for all have sinned, and fall short of the glory of God; being justified freely by his grace through the redemption that is in Christ Jesus* (Romans 3:21-24). So we are not made flawless by our works but by the work of Jesus on the cross. When King Balak called the Prophet Balam to put a curse on Israel, God didn't listen to Balam and the reason we come to know for this denial is, *"He has not seen iniquity in Jacob. Neither has he seen perverseness in Israel"* (Numbers 23:21). If there is no misfortune or misery observed in Israel, does it mean the whole Israelite community was so perfect that there wasn't any sin in any man? There could be sin in individuals but as a nation, there was no sin among them. In the same way, when God looks at the church, He sees it as a perfect one. He perfects us through His glory and Jesus Christ who lives in us (Ezekiel 16:14, John 17:23, Hebrews 10:14). Jesus is the only flawless person in this universe. By believing in Him we wear Christ, *"For as many of you as were baptized into Christ have put on Christ"* (Galatians 3:27). When we are clothed with Christ and God looks at us, He sees Jesus because we are hiding in Him. When He sees Jesus, He doesn't see any flaw in Him. So by hiding herself in Christ, the bride becomes flawless. Therefore Jesus said that you are altogether beautiful and flawless.

4:8

Come with me from Lebanon, my bride, with me from Lebanon. Look from the top of Amana, from the top of Senir and Hermon, from the lions' dens, from the mountains of the leopards.

Jesus is teaching his bride to trust Him. There was a time when Lebanon was a part of Israel. In ancient times, Lebanon was also known as "White Mountain" because of the snow there. Mount Hermon is still under Israeli control. It is a tourist attraction and covered with snow. Mountains are difficult to cross, especially when they are covered with snow. Roughness and steep heights make it difficult for anyone to climb. Many people can slip in the snow and injure themselves. Some people believe that it is the same mountain where the transfiguration of Jesus took place. First, these areas were under the control of Canaanites but later the Israelites from the tribe of Manasseh occupied the area and lived there.

As traveling in the hilly areas is sometimes difficult because of landslides, extreme weather, and wild animals, Jesus is telling His bride to trust and depend on Him to cross these areas and reach a safe place. Hills and mountains are the difficulties in our lives and wild animals who are ready to attack and devour are the enemies of the bride. Lions and leopards are two kinds of enemies mentioned in this verse; they represent physical and spiritual forces against us. Most of the time, besides the physical enemies or people against us, there are spiritual forces of darkness that come against us but they use humans as their tools. We see John the Baptist in the gospel of Matthew. He was preaching and baptizing the people. He was supposed to be polite with them but he used very strong words against the Pharisees. *But when he saw many of the Pharisees and Sadducees coming for his baptism, he said to them, "You offspring of vipers, who warned you to flee from the wrath to come?* (Matthew 3:7). Why did John the Baptist call them a "*offspring of vipers*"? He was revealing the actual working force behind the Pharisees. It looked like humans were standing there in the form of the Pharisees, but inside them, satanic forces were ruling. God opens our eyes to see the actual person working against us.

Jesus met a crippled woman in a synagogue. Outwardly, it appeared she was suffering from some disease, but Jesus saw the actual cause of sickness and that was an evil spirit. *He was teaching in one of the synagogues on the Sabbath day. Behold, there was a woman who had a spirit of infirmity eighteen years. She was bent over, and could in no way straighten herself up. When Jesus saw her, he called her, and said to her, "Woman, you are freed from your infirmity." He laid his hands on her, and immediately she stood up straight and glorified God* (Luke 13:10-13). Normally, we don't see evil spirits with our physical eyes. Similarly, people were not able to see evil spirits working amongst the Pharisees and in the crippled lady. They were not able to heal the sick by destroying the work of the enemy. We can't overcome the devil without Jesus. Therefore Jesus was encouraging the bride to stay with Jesus for her own safety; as the enemy is seeking the opportunity to devour anyone who comes in his range (1-Peter 5:8). Jesus knows it is difficult for us to tackle all the problems in life on our own. Therefore he encourages His bride to depend on Him and He will take us from the mountains and keep us safe from all the wild animals.

4:9

You have ravished my heart, my sister, my bride. You have ravished my heart with one of your eyes, with one chain of your neck.

At first, the bridegroom was praising the beauty of the bride. Later we see him praising her for the ornaments she is wearing. The ornaments match her personality like they are made specifically for her. But the question is, what kind of ornaments she is wearing and who has provided them? In Song of Songs 1:10-11, it is written, *"Your cheeks are beautiful with earrings, your neck with strings of jewels. We will make you earrings of gold, with studs of silver."* So it is clear that the ornaments the bride is wearing are gifted by the king. In Proverbs 16:15, it is written, *"In the light of the king's face is life. His favor is like a cloud of the spring rain"* When a king is happy with his servants or anyone he likes, he blesses them with gifts. Our king, Jesus Christ is happy with His bride, so He blesses her with different gifts. Along with other things, these gifts include ornaments which she is wearing, and they are contributing to her beauty. Although these gifts show the king's affection and love towards someone, at the same time royal ornaments show the royalty of a person. When Joseph was in jail, his dress, chains, and appearance showed that he was a prisoner but when Pharaoh exalted him, he gave him royal ornaments to show that he is a high ranking officer. In the same way, King Belshazzar rewarded Daniel with a high rank in the kingdom and a gold chain (Daniel 5:29). God deals with us in the same way. We were in the prison of sin but He took us out and washed us with His blood (Hebrews 1:3, Revelation 7:14). He gave us new dress and shoes (Ephesians 6:15), took us into the royal palace (Song of Songs 2:4, John 14:2-3), and blessed us with authority in this world over demons and in heaven, we will judge the angels (1-Corinthians 6:3).

In Ezekiel 16:10-12, God said, *"I clothed you also with embroidered work, and put sealskin sandals on you. I dressed you with fine linen and covered you with silk. I decked you with ornaments, put bracelets on your hands, and put a chain on your neck."* God was addressing Israel. The blessings mentioned in these verses have both spiritual and physical meanings but for now, we will take them spiritually. *Don't let kindness and truth forsake you. Bind them around your neck* (Proverbs 3:3). The same kind of instructions we find in Proverbs 6:20-21 about the teachings of the parents; these teachings are ornaments that increase our beauty. God is not impressed by the amount of physical jewelry someone is wearing but by how much we are faithful to the teachings of our physical and spiritual father. Love and faithfulness towards God and humans are the ornaments that God likes us to wear because we see the same qualities in the life of Jesus as well.

4:10

How beautiful is your love, my sister, my bride! How much better is your love than wine, the fragrance of your perfumes than all kinds of spices!

One of the difficult things to understand in the Song of Songs is why God allowed Solomon to call his wife his sister. According to Christian teachings, it is clear that a sister can't become the wife of her brother. God is a Spirit and He never needed a wife. God never had any sexual desires. The reason He allowed to Solomon write such a thing is that He wanted to express the purity and genuineness of His love and relationship with the church. The relationship between husband and wife is the most open relationship where you don't hide your feelings from each other. The relationship between a brother and sister is a pure form of love where you take care of each other and never cross the boundaries, ordained by God. The love of Jesus is the combination of both. He opens His heart to us and we open our hearts and hurts to Him. We can openly express our sorrows, worries, and happy moments with Him. The things which are difficult to express to our husband or wife, He already knows that we are going through those difficulties. As God already knows our condition, then it becomes easy to pour our hearts out before Him. In this way, He is closer than a husband or wife. At the same time, His love is so deep that He didn't care about His glory; He left His glory as God and came to earth as a common man. He selected a manger to be His birthplace. This was a place where animals used to live and give birth to their offspring. He was king of kings but led a simple life and died the death of a sinner although He was the only sinless man on the face of the earth. He rose again, gave power and authority to His brothers and sisters. After doing all this He never boasted against us. His love is purer than the love of any brother and sister. The words husband, wife, brother, or sister are used only to express closeness, care, purity, and the affection He has for His people. No matter how many beautiful or big words we may use, we will never be able to fully describe His great love. Our human mind is unable to comprehend the love of Christ. His love is like a mountain, different people climb this mountain from different sides. Each person will see the side from where he is climbing. At the end of the day, different people will come together and share the experience they had and we will learn through each other's experiences. This fact was better explained by Apostle Paul in Ephesians 3:14-19

For this cause, I bow my knees to the Father of our Lord Jesus Christ, from whom every family in heaven and on earth is named, that he would grant you, according to the riches of his glory, that you may be strengthened with power through his Spirit in the inner person, that Christ may dwell in your hearts through faith, to the end that you, being rooted and grounded in love, may be strengthened to comprehend with all the saints what is the width and length and height and depth, and to know Christ's love which surpasses knowledge, that you may be filled with all the fullness of God.

In the later part of the verse under consideration, He compares His love with the love of wine. Because of the intensity of His love,

He prefers the love and relationship more highly than wine. He compared her love with wine because no matter how rich or poor a man is, if he loves wine, his love for wine exceeds every other thing in the world. If you look at the life of an addict, you will see that he will value his addiction more than his friends or family. Jesus is saying that the love I have for you is stronger than any wine. He enjoys loving us more than a person who enjoys wine or any other strong drink.

It is the desire of every believer that we may stay in His presence. But against the desire we have for His presence, His desire for our presence is even stronger. When we talk about love, we often give an example of the love of a mother and child. A child always wants to be around his mother. Sometimes while playing, children become so obsessed with their games that they forget about their surroundings. Even if a child forgets to take care of, a mother never takes any risk about her child. She is always there for her child. Similarly, we may go away from God, but God is always around us. He is so near to us that He knows the perfumes we are using. We can only know this when we are in someone's presence. In this way, both the church and God desire each other's presence. Jesus prefers our perfume to any other valuable spice. It means He loves to stay with us more than we love to stay with Him.

4:11

Your lips, my bride, drip like the honeycomb. Honey and milk are under your tongue. The smell of your garments is like the smell of Lebanon.

Lips and tongues are associated with speech; aligning them with honeycomb, shows that the speech is purposeful and delighting. His bride, the church lives in this world. So the church has interaction with the world and with God. Our priority is our relationship with God. Our relationship with the world depends on the teachings we have in the Bible. We love God, and that love should be manifested in our dealing with the world. We see this love in Abraham and God's dealing with each other. Abraham was a friend of God (2-Chronicles 20:7, Isaiah 41:8, James 2:23). In Genesis 18, Jesus came to meet Abraham. First, they had been talking about Abraham's future, but later Jesus told him that He will destroy Sodom and Gomorrah. As soon as Abraham learned this, he started interceding for the people there. Intercession and worship are things enjoyed by God. He looks for people who intercede and worship (Isaiah 59:16, John 4:23). They are the people near to God's heart. The words of intercession and worship are like honeycomb to Jesus.

Milk and honey are the gifts of God that humans use as their food. The common thing about both is that they are not produced by human hard work, like rice, wheat, barley, etc. But, milk and honey are given to humans without much human interference. Honey is made by bees, they do all the hard work and humans get benefits from their work. Milk is produced by cattle and humans don't have to work for that. We may think that at least fodder is provided by humans but if you will just leave them in the open, they will find their food and still produce milk. Milk is good for infants but most of the doctors agreed that honey shouldn't be given to infants before the age of one year. Clostridium Botulinum bacteria can contaminate honey and can be dangerous for the infant's life. So milk can be taken in all ages but honey should only be taken by humans who are a bit stronger and can fight bacteria. The Word of God also has two sections; one is milk that is for both new and old believers. The other part of the spiritual food is honey or solid food, which means deeper truths of the Word. This is the food for grown-up believers. While writing to the believers in the epistle of Hebrews, Paul explained the difference between solid food and milk. *For everyone who lives on milk is not experienced in the word of righteousness, for he is a baby. But solid food is for those who are full grown, who by reason of use have their senses exercised to discern good and evil* (Hebrews 5:13-14). Milk and honey are both under the tongue of the bride. This means the bride can feed spiritual infants and mature believers. It is a good check for any pastor or preacher preparing the sermons for a common Sunday service. He shouldn't prepare his sermons only for mature believers but his speech should be effective for both. Jesus' teachings are still inspiring both new and mature believers.

Jesus said the fragrance of the garments of the bride is like the fragrance of Lebanon. Lebanon was one of the most beautiful areas in Israel. The beauty of Lebanon was recorded several times in the Bible. It was the land of high cedars, dew, and abundance of water (Jeremiah 18:14). It was a hilly country where the Amorites had been living before the Israelites took control (Deuteronomy 1:7). King Solomon built a palace in this area (1-Kings 7:2). In Hosea 14:5-7, God compared the beauty of Lebanon with Israel.

I will be like the dew to Israel. He will blossom like the lily, and send down his roots like Lebanon. His branches will spread, and his beauty will be like the olive tree, and his fragrance like Lebanon. Men will dwell in his shade. They will revive like the grain, and blossom like the vine. Their fragrance will be like the wine of Lebanon.

The fragrance of something reminds us of that thing; if we smell the fragrance of mangoes then our brain makes up the figure of mango in our imagination. When we talk about the fragrance of Lebanon, our mind sketches the beautiful scenery there, which reminds us of the abundance of God's blessings there. The abundance of water with suitable weather makes that land fertile. Similarly, when we say that from the garments of the bride we can smell the fragrance of Lebanon, it means when someone comes near the bride he will think about the abundance of God's supplies for His bride. Solomon figuratively made the relationship between the bride and the fragrance of her garments with Lebanon but God explained this mystery in detail in the book of Hosea.

The beauty of the bride is due to the mercy of God. She looks beautiful because God has washed away her sins and the ugliness of the sin is gone. God said that the fragrance of Israel will be like the fragrance of the cedars of Lebanon. It means His bride, His people, will flourish like the cedars of Lebanon. Their fame will spread like a fragrance. Everyone who will honor Israel will have God's blessing. Every country that will accept the shade or supremacy of His people, will flourish.

4:12

My sister, my bride, is a locked up garden; a locked up spring, a sealed fountain.

We have already discussed the issue of why the bride is called a sister in Song of Songs 4:9, so we will skip this portion in this verse. The bride is called a locked-up garden, enclosed spring, and a sealed fountain. All these terms have the same meaning that the bride has preserved herself only for the bridegroom. This is a truth which we need to apply in our common life as well. A husband and wife should keep themselves only for each other. We are not supposed to behave like public property. We shouldn't behave like a public bus where everyone is allowed to travel for a short while. We make promises with our spouses in the presence of God. When we make promises keeping God as our mediator, they become a covenant. If we break a covenant by breaking any of the promises then God judges between us and our partner (Malachi 2:14-16). When we go against the marriage covenant by breaking our vows, we go against God. *It is a fearful thing to fall into the hands of the living God* (Hebrews 10:31).

The bride is spoken of as a spring and fountain. Sometimes we see a spring but often there is a fountain that is supplying water to the spring. If you go and visit the source of River Jordan at the foot of Mount Hermon, you will see a spring but the water of that spring is coming from a fountain that is under the mountain. The bride is called an enclosed spring and a sealed fountain. Figuratively, God is also known by the same names. *They have forsaken me, the spring of living waters* (Jeremiah 2:13). *In that day there will be a spring opened to David's house and to the inhabitants of Jerusalem, for sin and for uncleanness* (Zechariah 13:1). Jesus is the fountain who cleanses sin. Jesus and the bride are both called spring and fountain. It means the characteristics God has are now found in the bride. One of the reasons why God keeps the church in this world is to show God's characteristics of love to the world. *But you are a chosen race, a royal priesthood, a holy nation, a people for God's own possession, that you may proclaim the excellence of him who called you out of darkness into his marvelous light* (1-Peter 2:9). *Having good behavior among the nations, so in that of which they speak against you as evildoers, they may by your good works, which they see, glorify God in the day of visitation* (1-Peter 2:12).

Before God chose us, we were like dry and barren land. When God blessed us with His forgiveness, He replaced our dryness with living waters. This living water comes out of Jesus and reaches everyone who accepts Him as His Saviour. This water becomes a spring in us which leads to eternal life (John 4:14). The source of this living water is God Himself. *"Those who sing as well as those who dance say, all my springs are in you"* (Psalm 87:7). This living water flows through the bride when believers preach the Word in and out of the church. This water brings blessings to everyone. The church flourishes like a garden, a garden where God comes to visit His people as He had been visiting in Eden. We enjoy the blessings of God, but the church is a garden where God enjoys His bride. He likes to walk in this garden in the cool of the day; this arouses the worship in the heart which bubbles up like a spring and a fountain.

4:13-14

Your shoots are an orchard of pomegranates, with precious fruits, henna with spikenard plants, spikenard and saffron, calamus and cinnamon, with every kind of incense tree; myrrh and aloes, with all the best spices,

The whole book of Song of Songs revolves around the love of Christ and the church. The people who love Him adore Him and the words of adoration become worship. When His people worship Him, His love wraps them in the form of anointing. Different people may explain differently about anointing but for me, anointing is the physical realization of the touch of the Holy Spirit. In short, we can say that our love for Christ initiates the Holy Spirit to work in us. When the Holy Spirit works in us, He works in two ways. He changes us in our character and through us, manifests His presence to others. When He works in us, He produces the fruits of the Holy Spirit. When He works through us, He manifests gifts of the Holy Spirit.

It is not a coincidence that there are nine gifts of the Holy Spirit and nine fruits. By studying carefully, we can see a one-to-one correlation between the fruits and the gifts of the Spirit. The gifts and fruits are both important to a believer. They are like feathers on each side of a pigeon. If the feathers on the left side are spiritual gifts then the feathers on the right side are spiritual fruits. If there are feathers on one wing of the pigeon and not on the other wing, the pigeon wouldn't be able to fly. To go high in the skies we need both the spiritual gifts and the fruits as our feathers. *But the fruit of the Spirit is love, joy, peace, patience, kindness, goodness, faith, gentleness, and self-control. Against such things there is no law* (Galatians 5:22-23). *Now there are various kinds of gifts, but the same Spirit. There are various kinds of service, and the same Lord. There are various kinds of workings, but the same God, who works all things in all. But to each one is given the manifestation of the Spirit for the profit of all. For to one is given through the Spirit the word of wisdom, and to another the word of knowledge, according to the same Spirit; to another faith, by the same Spirit; and to another gifts of healings, by the same Spirit; and to another workings of miracles; and to another prophecy; and to another discerning of spirits; to another different kinds of languages; and to another the interpretation of languages. But the one and the same Spirit produces all of these, distributing to each one separately as he desires* (1-Corinthians 12:4-11).

The list of fruits given in Song of Songs 4:13-14, can be divided into three categories. The words, "Your shoots are an orchard of pomegranates, with precious fruits" is the first category in which different fruits are included, the pomegranate is taken only as an example. These are the fruit trees that are good for human health. By these fruits, the church refreshes the people who are weary and burdened (Matthew 11:28). In the second category, some plants mentioned are used for different medicines and foods like saffron, cinnamon, and aloes. These are medicinal plants and can be used to heal different sicknesses. When people come with their sicknesses and diseases, church people pray for them and they can be healed. When the church takes care of the elderly, sick, and homeless; then the church is acting like medicine for many broken-hearted, as we see in the second category. In the third category, plants that were used in the temple for different rituals are mentioned. These are the plants that were used to make anointing oil and incense to burn on the altar, their basic purpose was to produce a pleasing aroma for God. The church is a blessing for the world but at the same time, the church is near to God's heart. Worship pleases the heart of God and a church leads the people into worship of God. It shows the work of the bride, explained in the third category. In Song of Songs 4:12, the bride was considered as a garden; in verses 13 and 14 the plants of that garden are discussed. By comparing the bride with different plants and trees, God told the purpose of the church on this earth.

The work of the Holy Spirit can be divided into three categories; just as we have already seen the division of the work of the church in three categories. The work of the Holy Spirit can be seen in our lives in the form of fruits and gifts of the Holy Spirit. Commonly, the gifts of the Holy Spirit are divided into three categories. The first category is known as, "gifts of knowledge". In this category, words of wisdom, words of knowledge, and distinguishing between spirits are included. The second category is, "gifts of speech", tongues, interpretation, and prophecy are included in this category. The third category is called, "gifts of power", faith, healing, and miracles are part of this group. Similarly, the fruits of the Holy Spirit can also be divided into three categories. Love, joy, and peace are in the first category. These are the fruits that help in building up the believer's spirit. These fruits bring patience and endurance in believers against all the unfavorable circumstances. In the second category, there are forbearance, kindness, and goodness. These are the fruits that help us in serving other people. While serving others, we need forbearance, kindness, and goodness to keep our morals high. In the third category, we see faithfulness, gentleness, and self-control. These fruits are needed to serve God. We need to serve God faithfully and gently. When God exalts us as a result of our service to Him, we need self-control that we may not boast about ourselves.

The three categories of the fruits of the Spirit very much correlate with the categories we saw in Song of Songs 4:13-14. Through Solomon, God was prophetically teaching about the fruits of the Holy Spirit. But, the fruits of the Holy Spirit are linked closely with the gifts of the Holy Spirit. The gifts of the Holy Spirit are powerful tools to serve God but these gifts can't work properly without the fruits of the Holy Spirit. So the gifts and fruits of the Holy Spirit help us to grow in the Spirit with proper balance, whereas the classification of the fruits given in Song of Songs 4:13-14 helps us to understand the purpose of the church on this earth. Please check the table on the next page.

Fruits mentioned In Song of Songs	Fruits of Spirit In Galatians	Gifts of Spirit In 1-Corinthians
First Category Pomegranates, fruits	**First Category** Love, joy, and peace	**First Category** Word of wisdom, word of wisdom, word of knowledge
Second Category Henna, nard, saffron, calamus, cinnamon (medicinal plants)	**Second Category** Forbearance, kindness, and goodness	**Second Category** Tongues, interpretation, and prophecy
Third Category Incense tree, myrrh and aloes (plants used in the temple)	**Third Category** Faithfulness, gentleness, self-control	**Third Category** Faith, healing, and miracles

4:15

a fountain of gardens, a well of living waters, flowing streams from Lebanon.

The church is a garden fountain. It is like a fountain by which the whole garden is watered; then its water goes out in the form of a stream to water other areas. As the fountain is in the garden so firstly the plants, or believers, in the garden would be supplied. They will be the plants that will never face the problem of water shortage.

Psalm 1 talks about the blessings of the man who is planted in the church, he is like a well-watered plant. *Blessed is the man who doesn't walk in the counsel of the wicked, nor stand on the path of sinners, nor sit in the seat of scoffers; but his delight is in Yahweh's law. On his law he meditates day and night. He will be like a tree planted by the streams of water, that produces its fruit in its season, whose leaf also does not wither. Whatever he does shall prosper* (Psalm 1:1-3). We are blessed because we are born in a time when God has ordained the church as a blessing for the world. The Old Testament believers never had access to the Word of God as freely as we have. In the time of Moses, the first five books of the Bible were written. It was the time when books were not available in paper or electronic format, people didn't have the legacy to keep the Word in their cell phones and carry it wherever they want. It was written on the heavy scrolls made of leather. The more we have access to the Word of God, the more people are walking away from it. As we have more resources than ever before, therefore our responsibility is increased. We must take the Word to the ends of this world.

The water from the fountain of the church is coming from Lebanon, which was one of the Israelite borders. *From the wilderness and this Lebanon even to the great river, the river Euphrates, all the land of the Hittites, and to the great sea toward the going down of the sun, shall be your border* (Joshua 1:4). The Bible mentions that the Israelite's territory was from the desert to Lebanon. Solomon said that the bride is like a fountain streaming from Lebanon. So the church's territory is from Lebanon to the desert (Song of Songs 4:15) because when a stream or fountain starts in the mountains, it goes towards the plains, passes through the desert, and ends up in the sea. Israelites' move is opposite to the church's move. Israelites moved from the desert to Lebanon and church moved from Lebanon to the desert. The Israelites were coming from the desert of Sinai and they were heading towards Lebanon. Whereas, the church is coming from Lebanon and going towards the desert; because we have found the love and satisfaction in Christ and we want to share this blessing with the dry world. Our high place or Lebanon is heaven, where Christ is; this is the place where the fountain of the church starts and comes to a lower place known as the world. Spiritually, the Israelites were lacking because they were waiting for the coming Messiah to take them from the scorching heat of the desert to the fertile and well-watered land of Lebanon; from the sand of the desert to the cool places of Lebanon and white snow; from the blood of animals to the blood of Christ. The Messiah will take them from hell to heaven. All the spirits of all the humans, including believers, had been going to a specific portion of hell, but after Jesus' sacrifice, believers' spirits started going to heaven. The believers of the Old Testament times were looking for a better future; that better future was Christ, himself. Christ established the church. Since Jesus established the church, people from different nations are coming and quenching their thirst from this spiritual river.

When any river ends up, it eventually flows into a larger body of water, like a sea. In Matthew 28:19 Jesus commanded his disciples to go into the world. In this way, the church which has the river of living water in itself, also ends up in the world. The world is full of malice, deceit, and all kinds of evil, but the church is giving its sweetness to remove the saltiness of the sea of the world. God in His infinite wisdom and love declared hundreds of years before the formation of the church that the church will bless the whole world. When God met the Prophet Ezekiel, He showed him in a vision that the water which was coming out of the temple will change the salt water of the sea into sweet water.

Ezekiel 47:6-12

He said to me, "Son of man, have you seen?" Then he brought me, and caused me to return to the bank of the river. Now when I had returned, behold, on the bank of the river were very many trees on the one side and on the other. Then he said to me, "These waters flow out toward the eastern region, and will go down into the Arabah. Then they will go toward the sea; and flow into the sea which will be made to flow out; and the waters will be healed. It will happen, that every living creature which swarms, in every place where the rivers come, will live. Then there will be a very great multitude of fish; for these waters have come there, and the waters of the sea will be healed, and everything will live wherever the river comes. It will happen, that fishermen will stand by it. From En Gedi even to En Eglaim will be a place for the spreading of nets. Their fish will be after their kinds, as the fish of the great sea, exceedingly many. But the miry places of it, and its marshes, will not be healed. They will be given up to salt. By the river on its bank, on this side and on that side, will grow every tree for food, whose leaf won't wither, neither will its fruit fail. It will produce new fruit every month, because its waters issue out of the sanctuary. Its fruit will be for food, and its leaf for healing."

Prophetically, God was describing the future ministry of the church through Ezekiel. We can find fish in rivers but not in the extremely salty water of the Dead Sea. Symbolically, God was saying that the extreme saltiness of the sin in this world would be changed by the sweet waters of life flowing through the church because Jesus would be working through the church in the form of living waters. People will find believers in the form of fish and the fishermen we see in this vision are the church planters, fisher of men who will gather the fish in the churches.

4:16

Awake, north wind, and come, you south! Blow on my garden, that its spices may flow out. Let my beloved come into his garden, and taste his precious fruits.

In the previous verse, the bridegroom called the bride a garden. Now the bride is requesting that the wind of God may blow on the garden. There are a lot of references about the wind in the Bible. Almost all the things mentioned in Songs of Songs are figurative.

Therefore we will study the figurative meanings of the wind in the Bible. In Luke 12:55, Jesus said, *"When a south wind blows, you say, 'There will be a scorching heat,' and it happens."* North winds and South winds help each other in changing the weather. The church doesn't only want to change the spiritual weather of the world that the world may accept Jesus as its savior; it also wants the spiritual weather inside the church to also be changed. The change of weather is like a revival that is constantly needed in the church. If there is no revival in the church, then the church behaves like stagnant water and often there is a bad smell from stagnant water. If you study the life of Jesus, throughout His ministry, like a wind. He was constantly moving from one place to another to preach the gospel. At different places, people were accepting His teachings. In this way, He was constantly seeing a revival in the lives of people. The same was the method of Paul the Apostle. After he accepted Christ, we see a constant move in his life; even when he was in prison, he never stopped preaching. The Israelites, the church of the Old Testament, kept on moving when they were in the wilderness and God's pillar of the fire remained with them. God doesn't want us to stick in one place or experience. We need to transform gradually. *Don't be conformed to this world, but be transformed by the renewing of your mind* (Romans 12:2). To get that transformation, the bride is requesting the wind to blow to change the spiritual atmosphere.

While reading about the heroes of faith, we sometimes think that they didn't go through the problems we are experiencing. James 5:17 says, *"Elijah was a man with a nature like ours"* He was a great prophet, but he also had times when he felt down and needed a revival. He was so depressed that he wanted to quit his ministry, and even his life, but God revived him on Mount Horeb (1-Kings 19:1-14). He encountered God there and came back revived. That revival in his life was so strong that it continued even after his life in the form of double anointing on the life of Elisha. At the very last moment of his earthly life, he saw a new revelation and experience that never happened before and has not been seen since.

The experience of transformation and fiery chariots has never been repeated. The last revival in the life of Elijah became a new revival in the life of Elisha. That revival benefited the whole nation because the nation of Israel gained a new prophet. We can say that the new prophet was even powerful than the previous one, the new prophet performed twice the miracles performed by the previous one. The more we have the desire for God, the stronger the revival will be. Elisha requested double the anointing Elijah had and he got it. You can ask God and He can send an even greater revival in your time than ever before.

The bride asked for a fresh move of the Holy Spirit by asking for the wind of the Holy Spirit to blow on her garden. The love of the bride is so perfect that she doesn't want her exaltation or pleasure. The only thing she wants from the move of the wind is the visitation of her beloved. She wants to attract Christ through the scent which will spread by the blowing of the wind. This wind is the wind of the Holy Spirit; it means the wind of the Holy Spirit spreads the perfume by which Jesus is attracted. The Holy Spirit knows Jesus like a best friend. No one else knows Jesus better than the Holy Spirit. So when the Holy Spirit moves in the church in the form of wind, He knows how to attract Jesus. The Holy Spirit being on our side is a plus point for us. Jesus is attracted by the worship of the believers; this is the scent that rises to heaven. Jesus comes where believers worship Him, even if the sound of the worship is coming from jail. When Jesus was attracted by their worship, He came into their midst and released them (Acts 16:22-28, 5:17-24). This should be the desire of every believer that He may come into His garden, into the church. When He comes, demons flee away and the sick are healed. The fruit from the garden of the bride which the bridegroom likes is mentioned in Hebrews 13:15, *"Through him, then, let's offer up a sacrifice of praise to God continually, that is, the fruit of lips which proclaim allegiance to his name."* When the wind of the Holy Spirit blows on our gardens (our spirits), worship comes out from our innermost being and this is the fruit He likes from the garden of His bride.

5

5:1

I have come into my garden, my sister, my bride. I have gathered my myrrh with my spice; I have eaten my honeycomb with my honey; I have drunk my wine with my milk. Eat, friends! Drink, yes, drink abundantly, beloved.

It seems that the bridegroom and His friends are in a banquet hall where there is spread an array of choice foods. Spiritually, we can't confuse this banquet with the marriage supper of the lamb because in the later verses of this chapter we see a kind of disagreement between the bride and the bridegroom (Revelation 19:7). The groom, in this verse, looks very happy. He tells His bride that He has gathered the myrrh and spice; each of these items has significance. Myrrh was an essential part of the life of a priest because it was extensively used in the temple for worship purposes. In place of spice in some translations, the word "balsam" is used. This word is used in Genesis 37:25, Jeremiah 46:11, 51:8. Mostly, the places where the word "balsam (spice)" is used, it talks about healing. Honey and honeycomb have great health benefits but they represent the Word of God (Psalm 19:10). The taste of Manna was like honey (Exodus 16:31). Honey was a trading commodity as well. The wine was used in sacrificial rituals (Numbers 15:5). Wine may have some health benefits when we use it responsibly but here we are not advocating the use of wine. We are looking at spiritual aspects and meanings of different things in this verse. The other notable thing in this verse is the use of the word "my". My garden, my bride, my myrrh, my spice, my honeycomb, my honey, my wine, and my milk. It means everything belongs to Jesus and He provides for His followers. Whereas in Luke 9:55, John 11:11, and John 15:14-15 He calls His followers His friends. He is offering his friends His myrrh, spice (balsam), milk, wine, honey, and honeycomb. When myrrh is offered to Christ, it represents worship but when it is offered by Christ, it represents appreciation and earthly blessings. So Jesus is saying that He has provided everything to His bride and friends. He has provided His blood (balsam/ spices) for our healing. For our spiritual needs, He has given us His Word (honey). For spiritual children, He gave us spiritual milk.

One question which occurs to most people is why the bridegroom has called the bride His sister. When we look at the Word of God, we find two people who called their wives their sisters. Abraham (Genesis 12:13-15, 20:2-12) and Isaac (Genesis 26:7). When Abraham was asked by the king why he called his wife his sister, he said that his wife was the daughter of his father and not his mother (Genesis 20:12). In this way, although she is my wife from my father's side she is my sister as well. Maybe for some people, this justification is not enough but the interesting fact is that God didn't blame him for any sin in this whole incident. Keeping in mind the reason Abraham gave, let's read Hebrews 2:11.

For both he who sanctifies and those who are sanctified are all from one, for which cause he is not ashamed to call them brothers.

Jesus came from God (John 8:42, 16:27-28). All humans are made by God. So, common people and Jesus both came from God. The writer of Hebrews in 2:11 says that Jesus is not ashamed of naming His followers as His brothers and sisters because the source of both is the same, God. Although Sara was Abraham's wife, he called her, his sister because he and his sister both came into this world from the same source, their earthly Father. In the same way,

Jesus the bridegroom calls His beloved His sister because both bride (church) and bridegroom have the same source, God.

5:2

I was asleep, but my heart was awake. It is the voice of my beloved who knocks: "Open to me, my sister, my love, my dove, my undefiled; for my head is filled with dew, and my hair with the dampness of the night."

We see two people who are in different conditions. The bride is sleeping and the bridegroom is awake. The bridegroom is longing to see His bride. His head is drenched with dew. In almost all the Bible references about dew, we see that dew is a blessing of God (Genesis 27:28, Numbers 11:9, Deuteronmy 33:28). But, here we see that dew is showing something different than a blessing. First, it is showing that the bridegroom is waiting for the response of the bride for many hours. Someone's head can only be drenched with dew if he is waiting for a long time in the open. Secondly, it shows that it was the winter season when He was waiting outside because usually, it is winter in the Middle East when there is a lot of dew. We can see the negligence of the bride and faithfulness of the bridegroom; He had been waiting some hours, in the cold. Instead of answering the door, the bride was asleep. This shows not only the negligence of the bride but the hours of the persistence of the bridegroom.

Jesus knocks on the heart of people. Whenever people ignore the inner voice of God, they fall into trouble. Jesus knew that if He left the bride because of her negligent behavior the bride would be in trouble. Although her behavior is not good Jesus is faithful to ensure her safety and wellbeing. If we look at the bride in present days, we can see many churches where Jesus is not in the church, He is standing outside and knocking on the door, waiting for someone to open the door. Many believers say that although we are not going to church; we are not giving our offerings; our time; our interest, or our will to Jesus. But this is the condition of a lukewarm person. In Revelation 3:14-18, He says that He will spit out such people.

When Jesus was in Gethsemane, He asked His disciples to stay awake and be in prayer with Him. But, the disciples were tired and wanted to sleep. He came to them again and again, but they were not able to see the need at the time (Mark 14:32-42). The crucifixion of Christ happened in winter (John 18:18). He was praying in the open, in a garden. His head must be drenched in dew; as it was winter (John 18:18). He was coming again and again to His bride but His bride (disciples) was not listening to Him. He already described their condition in Song of Solomon 5:2 that the heart of the bride is awake but the bride herself is sleeping. In Mark 14:38, He described the same condition by saying, *"The spirit indeed is willing, but the flesh is weak"*. Here disciples are the bride, struggling to keep their eyes open as Jesus faithfully persists. Jesus loves to spend time with His bride. He knew that He will be crucified the next day. He knew He will die in the next few hours. These were the last hours of Jesus' life. It was like the desire of a dying person. His desire was to spend time with His bride and God. So we can imagine how much deeper love He has for His bride that He wanted to spend the last hours with His bride, His disciples. There are churches and individuals as well who don't have Jesus at the center of their gatherings and Jesus is grieved about this fact. Yet He still sanctifies the church as His house. There is a big question for believers today. They have to judge themselves to discern whether Jesus is inside them or He is knocking at their door? Do we have a heart for Jesus or we are busy with our schedule? For everyone who is spiritually asleep, Jesus is knocking on the door, for hours, with dew on His head.

5:3-4

I have taken off my robe. Indeed, must I put it on? I have washed my feet. Indeed, must I soil them? My beloved thrust his hand in through the latch opening. My heart pounded for him.

The bride tells the reason why she was not opening the door. She is thinking of her comfort but she is not thinking of the hard circumstances in which the bridegroom was. She thinks that if I will get up to open the door, her feet will touch the ground and become dusty then she would have to wash them. She has taken off her robe and now she is enjoying her nap in a cozy bed. As we saw in Song of Solomon 5:2, from the description of dew, it seems it is a winter's night. On a cold winter's night, once you are in your bed, you wouldn't like to come out of it. These days we have heaters in our homes and dense carpets to keep our feet from touching the cold floor but in ancient times such facilities were not available. If the bride would leave her bed she has to bear the cold floor, then before returning to bed she must wash her feet with water which could be ice cold as well. When she thinks of all these things, she doesn't want to leave her comfort zone. But at the same time, she is ignoring the bridegroom who has come from far in the harsh winter weather. He is standing at the door of His own house like a stranger. It certainly gives an awkward feeling, especially when people are passing by and they can see that He is not being allowed into the house. In the first verse of this chapter, we see that the bridegroom came with His friends and arranged a party for His friends. It looks like it is a wedding party in which the bridegroom provided everything. When the party was finished, He came to His bride. He came to His bride, now it is a humiliating situation for the bridegroom in front of His friends; the bride is not opening the door for Him. In Song of Songs 2:17, we see that the bride is requesting the bridegroom to come to her before the darkness of night starts. The bridegroom has accepted the request of the bride but when He came to meet her, she is not opening the door for Him. It is a kind of humiliating situation the bridegroom is going through. The bridegroom is in a far more difficult situation than the bride. Hebrews 12:1-3 says,

Therefore let's also, seeing we are surrounded by so great a cloud of witnesses, lay aside every weight and the sin which so easily entangles us, and let's run with perseverance the race that is set before us, looking to Jesus, the author and perfecter of faith, who for the joy that was set before him endured the cross, despising its shame, and has sat down at the right hand of the throne of God. For consider him who has endured such contradiction of sinners against himself, that you don't grow weary, fainting in your souls.

The Church (bride) is surrounded by many witnesses. These witnesses are observing our behavior with Christ. So we need to be careful of our actions and deeds. We have to ignore every obstacle and open every door which is becoming a hindrance in our relationship with Christ. Jesus accepted a death which was horrible and didn't think of His great status and difficulties in this way. We should be bold like Christ, even if it looks foolish to the people around us.

When the bride didn't open the door, the bridegroom touched the latch opening. These days when you go to someone's house, if your friend is not at home, you usually leave your gift at the door with a visiting card. When your friend comes home, he will know about your coming by your card. In ancient times, when a friend came to the house and the house owner was not at home, the visitor used to anoint the latch opening with his perfume. When the house owner came back, he knew by the smell that his friend had come to visit him. In the same way, when the bridegroom saw that bride did not open the door, He touched the latch. Then the bride knew that it was Jesus who was waiting for her.

There are times in our lives when we don't care that God is calling us and we like to keep on going with our own purposes. If we keep on neglecting His knocks, which are different warnings about our lifestyle, then a time comes when Jesus leaves us in our busy schedule. Our constant ignorance of His warnings can leave us in spiritual darkness.

There are many incidences recorded in the Bible about the knocking of God. When they denied listening to Him, He left His mark, His word (His fragrance) on their door latch, and left them. He respects our free will. He had been warning King Saul and King Solomon about their wrongdoings, when they didn't listen, God left them alone. The dark side of being left alone by God is that we become open to Satan. Satan always waits for such a moment (Genesis 4:7). When the spirit of God left King Saul, an evil spirit came and started tormenting Saul. When the spirit of God was with Saul, no devil dared to come near Saul (1-Samuel 16:14-15). Similarly, we see that the Spirit of the Lord left Samson when he didn't take care of the Word of God and allowed his head to be shaved (Judges 16:1-21). Today we need to hear the call of Christ if He is knocking at our door.

5:5

I rose up to open for my beloved. My hands dripped with myrrh, my fingers with liquid myrrh, on the handles of the lock.

Myrrh had its different uses in the tabernacle. One of its uses was when the high priest had to go from holy place to the holy of holies. The incense had to be burnt there in the censer (Leviticus 16:12) and myrrh was part of the incense. In the previous verse when the bridegroom touched the door latch, the bride's emotions for her groom arose and compelled her to open the door. In Song of Solomon 4:6, the bridegroom said that He lives on the mountain of myrrh. It means He likes myrrh and wanted to give a second chance to His bride. He wants his bride to come and meet Him on the mountain of myrrh. When myrrh came out of the fingers of the bride, it means the bride is producing something which is liked by the groom. The myrrh is produced in different ways by the bride.

When we use our hands in worship, by playing the instruments in His praise, the myrrh is dripping by our fingers. When Israelites used to bring different sacrifices to God, these were acts of worship. Their hands and fingers were used in that worship. This was the myrrh dripping from their fingers. The proof that He accepted that worship/ myrrh is the anointing we see as a result of those sacrifices. Sometimes we don't see any *move* of God in our meetings. It means myrrh is not dripping out of the fingers. This shows some hindrance between Christ and the Church. The hindrance between us and Christ can't be removed simply. Sin is the hindrance between Him and us. He gave His life to remove that hindrance. He did whatever He had to do. Now we must step forward and open the door for Him. The door of our heart has *its'* bolts inside. Christ can't and will not open it from outside. Myrrh is the key that can open the door but it should flow from us as it flowed from the fingers of the bride.

5:6

I opened to my beloved; but my beloved left, and had gone away. My heart went out when he spoke. I looked for him, but I didn't find him. I called him, but he didn't answer.

The bride opened the door for the bridegroom but it was too late. From Song of Songs 5:2, we come to know that the head of the bridegroom was drenched with dew. It means He was waiting there for a long time. The patience of God is much more than humans but here we see that it is not forever. We see this in the Old Testament with how God related to the Israelites. He bought His people (the Israelites) to the land of milk and honey. In all that time He had been bearing them, teaching them, and disciplining them. When they entered Canaan, they followed God only in the time of Joshua and elders (Joshua 24:31). After Joshua, different judges reigned over the country for three hundred years (Judges 11:26), and after this, a long era of kings started in Israel (1000-587 BCE). Most of the time in the era of judges and kings, Israelites didn't follow God but God continued to send His prophets to them. He was knocking on their door through prophets but most of the prophets were mistreated by Israelites and some were killed (Matthew 16:21, 21:35, 23:35). It was the disobedience of His people (bride) that He left them on their own (2-Kings 23:27, 24:3, 24:20). When people cried out to God in Egypt, He rescued them but when they locked the doors of their hearts by continued disobedience, God removed Himself from them, as God moved Him away, the protection of Israel also removed from their heads. To discipline them He sometimes allowed invaders to afflict them but whenever Israelites cried to God, he delivered them. Other nations had been attacking Israel but Israelites remained in their land. When they were continuously disobeying the Lord, God allowed Babylon not only to attack but to take them out of their land, in exile in Babylon. They went into the slavery of Babylon. God never wanted to leave His people but when He waited for them for hundreds of years in the time of Judges and kings and they never wanted to come to Him, he was left with no other option but to leave them in the joys of their heart.

God doesn't want to leave his people because He knows that their protection and wellbeing depend on Him. By looking at the life of Joseph, we read again and again that God was with him. In all the afflictions of Jacob, God was with him. God was with Abraham. God gave his wife back to him from kings. He helped him in fighting with kings. He renewed his youth and gave him a son. God always stays with his people in their sorrows and joys. Our God is gentle. He didn't force the bride to open the door. He gently knocks. If he leaves us, we should be worried. David heard that knock when Prophet Nathan came to him and scolded him for sinning. David did wrong by killing Uriah the Hittite and by taking his wife, David became fearful and sorrowful. He asked for forgiveness. No matter what sin we did, we need to reconcile with God otherwise the results of our rudeness will be devastating like it was with King Saul.

After opening the door and seeing that bridegroom was not there, the bride became worried. She tried to look for Him but she didn't find Him. She even called Him but He didn't answer. Sometimes we think that God is so merciful that no matter what we do, He will accept us. We need to learn that God is merciful but at the same time He is a just God and He serves justice. We should be excited about His love but we should be aware of His justice as well. Sometimes because of our sins, He hides from us (Proverbs 1:24-29). In Hebrews 12:16-17, it is written,

Lest there be any sexually immoral person, or profane person, like Esau, who sold his birthright for one meal. For you know that even when he afterward desired to inherit the blessing, he was rejected, for he found no place for a change of mind though he sought it diligently with tears.

Paul uses the example of Esau. Esau first despised his birthright and sold it for a single meal. Later he sought that blessing with tears but he wasn't accepted. Just like Esau sold his birthright for a bowl of soup, the bride sold her life with the bridegroom for some more time in bed! And the disciples sold their time with Jesus before the crucifixion, for a few extra hours of sleep! This is truly where the 'flesh is weak'. Disciples preferred their nap over prayer. After some time when a multitude came to arrest Jesus in Gethsemane, they were not able to stand with Him. They all ran away, leaving Him alone. A while ago Jesus was asking them to stay with Him but they didn't value the time when Jesus was calling them. When temptation came, all of them fell in trouble. If we don't stay in prayer, we wouldn't be able to stay when trouble comes.

One week before His crucifixion, Jesus came to Jerusalem on a donkey but religious leaders there didn't value Him. He wept over Jerusalem. He prophesied against it and said that Jerusalem would be destroyed. He was not happy to utter such words; He was weeping at that time. But it was the decision of the Jewish leaders and people that led them to destruction. Jesus just informed them about the upcoming destruction in the form of prophecy. This prophecy was fulfilled in 70 AD. He gave the reason for that destruction. He said,

When he came near, he saw the city and wept over it, saying, "If you, even you, had known today the things which belong to your peace! But now, they are hidden from your eyes. For the days will come on you, when your enemies will throw up a barricade against you, surround you, hem you in on every side, and will dash you and your children within you to the ground. They will not leave in you one stone on another, because you didn't know the time of your visitation" (Luke 19:41-44). When we don't listen to Jesus, we open ourselves for destruction. Jesus came to His bride and knocked on the door. She didn't care for His love. He left her alone. Later when she realized all this, He was not there anymore.

5:7

The watchmen who go about the city found me. They beat me. They bruised me. The keepers of the walls took my cloak away from me.

Jesus is our protection from sickness, disease, and disappointment. When the bride didn't care for Christ, He left her alone. When watchmen found her alone, they beat her, misbehaved, and took away her cloak. They left her bruised. Mostly, watchmen symbolize religious leaders who are appointed to feed His people with spiritual food, but many times instead of feeding the spiritual children of God, they try to gather physical stuff for their biological children. In this process, they hurt His church; then we hear the news that some bishop or pastor misused the church funds, property, or authority. Many people are hurt by hearing such news. They are the watchmen who are supposed to be the protector of the bride but they are the ones who are hurting the church more than anyone else.

Sometimes religious leaders deal with people like commodities and use them for their own benefit. In this way, they hurt the flock. When David took the wife of Uriah the Hittite God said, "*However, because by this deed you have given great occasion to Yahweh's enemies to blaspheme, the child also who is born to you will surely die"* (2-Samuel 12:14). Being a king, David was a watchman for his people but his act bought shame on Israel. When a leader brings shame to his family, office, or country, it is like someone is it taking away the clothes or veil of his people. Watchmen misbehaved with the bride because the bride lost her connection with the bridegroom. In this way, it was not only the watchmen who were guilty but also the bride because the bridegroom wanted to be with the bride but the bride didn't care about His pure emotions. If the bridegroom had been with His bride, He would have been able to protect her from every evil.

Isaiah 46:3-4

Listen to me, house of Jacob, and all the remnant of the house of Israel, that have been carried from their birth, that have been carried from the womb. Even to old age I am he, and even to gray hairs I will carry you. I have made, and I will bear. Yes, I will carry, and will deliver.

John 10:27-29

My sheep hear my voice, and I know them, and they follow me. I give eternal life to them. They will never perish, and no one will snatch them out of my hand. My Father who has given them to me is greater than all. No one is able to snatch them out of my Father's hand.

If we are with Jesus, He will carry us. He took Israel when it was born. When He called Abraham, He gave him, Isaac and Jacob. This was the time of the birth of the nation Israel. When they grew, they occupied Canaan. Later they had their kings; it was the time of Israel's youth. He had been carrying the whole nation of Israel up till now. He promised that He will carry them till the end. When a father carries his child, no one can hurt that child. This promise of protection wasn't only with the nation of Israel; it is with all the believers. In the New Testament, Jesus called His people His sheep. No one has the power to snatch His sheep from Him. If the bride needs real protection, love, and safety, His bride should listen to Him and open the door whenever He calls her.

5:8

I adjure you, daughters of Jerusalem, If you find my beloved, that you tell him that I am faint with love.

In Song of Solomon 5:6, the bride called the bridegroom but He didn't answer. Now she is seeking help from "daughters of Jerusalem". Jerusalem means, "City of Peace". Daughters of Jerusalem mean the people who are living in the "city of peace". Spiritually speaking, she is asking help from other believers. Intercessors have the duty to pray for the people who are away from God. She is requesting the prayer team to help her. She desires that her request may be known by the king through the daughters of Jerusalem. By saying that *"I am faint with love"*, she is saying that if I will not find Him, I will be dying.

Many times, when God was angry with Israel, Moses interceded for them. He acted as the daughters of Jerusalem. In the same way, the Israelites sinned against God by asking for a king to rule them. God was king over Israel but they rejected God as their king.1-Samuel 12:19, *All the people said to Samuel, "Pray for your servants to Yahweh your God, that we not die; for we have added to all our sins this evil, to ask for a king."*

When the Israelites realized how big their sin was, they requested Samuel to intercede for them. Although God was angry with His people, He listened to Samuel. The bride knew that she didn't behave well with the bridegroom so she is requesting other believers to intercede for her. In Joel 1:14, the prophet Joel supports the idea of interceding for the nation so that God may accept His people again in His mercy.

5:9

How is your beloved better than another beloved, you fairest among women? How is your beloved better than another beloved, that you do so adjure us?

The daughters of Jerusalem admitted that the bride is the most beautiful of the women. In the Bible, mostly the word "women/woman" represent different nations (Isaiah 47:5-7, Lamentations 1:1). So, Christ's bride is the most beautiful among the nations of this world. The beauty of the bride is not physical. Christ likes His bride because she has Christ's attributes. His bride represents His attitude and attributes on this earth. 1-Peter 2:9, "*But you are a chosen race, a royal priesthood, a holy nation, a people for God's own possession, that you may proclaim the excellence of him who called you out of darkness into his marvelous light.*"

The love He has for His people is not because the Israelites were a strong nation. There were many strong nations when God chose a small and weak nation. He didn't start with a strong nation with a lot of resources. He started with a weak-man, Abraham, and from him made him a big nation (Deuteronomy 7:7).

Deuteronomy 4:37-38

Because he loved your fathers, therefore he chose their offspring after them, and brought you out with his presence, with his great power, out of Egypt; to drive out nations from before you greater and mightier than you, to bring you in, to give you their land for an inheritance, as it is today.

God himself made His people beautiful (Ezekiel 16:14). In the Old Testament, God made Israel beautiful and in the New Testament, Christ made the church beautiful. He offered the bride ornaments to look beautiful (Revelation 3:18). The beauty and appreciation His people have come when we act on His commandments

(Deuteronomy 4:6). This is the beauty towards which nations are attracted (Isaiah 60:3). So the daughters of Jerusalem asked the most beautiful woman about her beloved. They asked about the characteristics of her beloved. Everyone in some form or other has their beloved. For some people, their job is their beloved. For others, it could be money, power, games on cell phones, a TV program, any individual, or some targets in life. And everyone knows about his beloved! Women asked the bride about the qualities of her beloved. 1-Peter 3:15 says, "..... *Always be ready to give an answer to everyone who asks you a reason concerning the hope that is in you*". When women asked the bride about her beloved, she happily answered them in the following verses of this chapter. As Peter said, we need to be ready to answer everyone about our hope, our beloved Jesus Christ.

5:10

My beloved is white and ruddy. The best among ten thousand.

In ancient Israel "radiant and ruddy" or "red and white" are the words to describe the fairness and youth of someone. In 1-Samuel 16:12 the first appearance of David is described as, "*he was ruddy, with a handsome face and good appearance*". The words "white/ radiant and ruddy" describe the health of the bridegroom. It is a common saying that the health of a man is known for his fairness or color. So the bride is saying that her groom is perfect in His health. We know that Jesus had been healing many from their severe diseases. He was the one through whom healing power came out and touched others (Luke 6:19, 8:46). So He can't be affected by any disease. Instead, He is the one who can heal all the effects of every disease.

He is outstanding among ten thousand. Usually, there were ten thousand soldiers in a legion. It means He is prominent among the whole legion. He is better than all the men in the garrison. He is the one who created the hosts of heaven and earth (Genesis 2:1). Being a creator He is prominent above all of His creation. When David won the battle against Goliath, he became prominent not only in the army but also in the whole country. Jesus is the captain of the Lord's hosts. He appeared to Joshua when he was near Jericho, with a drawn sword in His hand. Joshua asked Him, *"Are you for us or for our enemies"?* (Joshua 5:13). Jesus gave him a very interesting answer. In Joshua 5:14 His answer is described as, *"No; but I have come now as commander of Yahweh's army."* The word "No" in the answer of Jesus shows that He is far above our thoughts. He was telling Joshua that He is greater than the armies of the enemy and the armies of Israelites. He is greater than all prophets and anyone in the universe. Hebrews 3:3, *"For he has been counted worthy of more glory than Moses, because he who built the house has more honor than the house."*

For Jews, the temple was the most respected and holy place on earth. It was respected more than any human on the earth. Jesus declared that He is more worthy of respect than the temple. Jesus explained that the sacrifices Jews used to bring were made holy at the altar. The altar was holy because it was in the temple. There were other altars outside the temple (for different gods) but they were not considered holy. The altar was making the sacrifices holy, and the altar was holy because it was in the temple and was used for God. But, God was the one who made the altar and the temple holy. So, God's holiness is much more than anything on the earth. Jesus is God; He is the one who makes everything holy. Being the holiest person, He is prominent and outstanding among thousands and thousands.

I tell you that one greater than the temple is here (Matthew 12:6).

... someone greater than Jonah is here (Matthew 12:41).

... someone greater than Solomon is here (Matthew 12:42).

5:11

His head is like the purest gold. His hair is bushy, black as a raven.

His head is purest gold. Head as purest gold represents purest thoughts. The thought He has for us is for our prosperity. *For I know the thoughts that I think toward you, says Yahweh, thoughts of peace, and not of evil, to give you hope and a future* (Jeremiah 29:11). *How precious to me are your thoughts, God! How vast is their sum!* (Psalm 139:17).

Black hair represents strength and youth. He has pure thoughts of love and prosperity for us, along with the power to fulfill them. Sometimes corruption comes in our thoughts. So we leave Him or hurt His pure feelings. But, He never changes His thoughts for us. Judas the Iscariot followed Jesus but later corruption came into his thoughts. The devil made his way into him through his mind (John 13:27). Jesus already knew from the beginning that who will betray Him (John 13:18-19) but He never decreased His love for him. He kept on loving him and the other disciples until the end (John 13:1).

He expressed His pure thoughts to His servant Abraham. He expressed the plan he had for the whole world. When God said that you will be the father of many nations (Genesis 17:4-5) that means many nations will come to God through Abraham. He expressed these thoughts of salvation for the whole world to Abraham and later He implemented those thoughts by sending His son in this world. So His purest thoughts came to pass through the purest man, Jesus Christ.

5:12

His eyes are like doves beside the water brooks, washed with milk, mounted like jewels.

In Song of Solomon 4:1, Solomon said his beloved had eyes like a dove. In the above verse, the bride said that her bridegroom has dove eyes. The bride and bridegroom both have the same kind of eyes. It means both of them are looking at things from the same perspective. For a successful relationship, it is the key element that both people have similar kinds of thoughts. Apostle Paul said, "*Don't be unequally yoked with unbelievers, for what fellowship do righteousness and iniquity have? Or what fellowship does light have with darkness?"* (2-Corinthians 6:14). These words are very true for people who want to be married. It is better to marry a believer instead of an unbeliever. Believers and unbelievers have different thoughts. Often they can't go together for a long distance. Therefore it is better to choose a partner who has the same kind of thoughts as you have like the bride and the bridegroom in the Song of Songs. In this way, they will move in the same spirit. For the Israelite leaders, God put the same spirit that Moses had in seventy elders, so that they may act in accordance with each other and with the Word of God. Now they had the same vision as Moses had for the nation. Because the Israelites' leaders/ elders had the same spirit as Moses, they were able to stand strong with Moses against the people, and not be cowed by greater numbers. That same spirit or vision empowered Israelite's elder to follow Moses when he went to talk with his opponents (Numbers 16:25).

The bride told about her beloved that His eyes are washed in milk, mounted like jewels. This phrase talks about the purity Jesus has in His look and the preciousness of that look. Jesus met with a Samaritan woman and he also met another woman when he was eating in the house of Simon the leper (Matthew 26:7, John 4:7). Neither of the women was considered as women of good character.

Jesus didn't take advantage of their loss of character or bad impact in society. Instead of their impurity, He looked at the purity they can have. Jesus forgave their sins and made them white as snow (Isaiah 1:18). By accepting the Word of God through Jesus, their changed life has been changing the lives of people throughout the world for two thousand years. Their story will never lose its' effectiveness until the end of the world (Matthew 26:13).

Being the bride of Christ, we need to have the same standard of love Jesus had in His eyes. We need not judge people by their outward appearance or past. We need to look to the future when people will walk in purity after gaining salvation. When Jesus forgives someone, He erases the sins from their lives like they were never there. In the same way, we need to see as Jesus sees and does not recall the sins of people again and again.

5:13

His cheeks are like a bed of spices with towers of perfumes. His lips are like lilies, dropping liquid myrrh.

Cheeks are an important part of our bodies. They show our inner feelings to others. Our facial impressions of joy or anger appear on our cheeks. Flower beds are normally a little bit raised above the normal ground level. His cheeks are raised like flower beds, for some people raised cheeks are a sign of beauty. For the bride, He is beautiful. His cheeks are like flowerbeds which are spreading the sweet smell of spice. Spices or balsam were used for healing, medicinal purpose, perfumes, and taste in food. His cheeks are yielding perfumes of spices. The smell of spices is used for different purposes. Some people use them during meditation. The smell of spices produces an effect on the mind which helps in meditation.

Spiritually, His face talks about a favor for His people. A common phrase, "may God shine His face on you" means that may God give you favor in your work and life. The blessing God asked the priests to pronounce on Israelites in Numbers 6:24-27, says again and again that God may shine His face upon His people. To stay in the glory of His face is a blessing for His people.

His lips are like lilies dripping with myrrh. Lilies describe the beauty of the lips. Myrrh comes out of His lips means His word is like myrrh. In Song of Songs 5:5, it is written that when myrrh fell on the lock, it was opened. When the myrrh comes out of the mouth of Jesus, it opens the lock of hearts. Myrrh has healing characteristics. The words of Jesus healed a lot of people.

When evening came, they brought to him many possessed with demons. He cast out the spirits with a word, and healed all who were sick (Matthew 8:16).

Therefore I didn't even think myself worthy to come to you; but say the word, and my servant will be healed (Luke 7:7).

The myrrh in the form of Word is a light unto our path (Psalm 119:105).

5:14

His hands are like rings of gold set with beryl. His body is like ivory work overlaid with sapphires.

Gold speaks about divinity. It is an expensive metal. Arms as rods of gold show the firmness of metal. His arms are strong and form an expensive secure environment around us. No one can cross that shield of protection around us. None of the weapons can penetrate through that shield.

Psalm 91:1-7

He who dwells in the secret place of the Most High will rest in the shadow of the Almighty. I will say of Yahweh, "He is my refuge and my fortress; my God, in whom I trust." For he will deliver you from the snare of the fowler, and from the deadly pestilence. He will cover you with his feathers. Under his wings you will take refuge. His faithfulness is your shield and rampart. You shall not be afraid of the terror by night, nor of the arrow that flies by day, nor of the pestilence that walks in darkness, nor of the destruction that wastes at noonday. A thousand may fall at your side, and ten thousand at your right hand; but it will not come near you.

His arms are decorated with topaz. In some Bible translations, instead of topaz, the word "beryl" is used. Individually, both stones come in different colors. Different colors show different talents a person may have. So Jesus Christ is the man of multiple talents. His talents/abilities or colors are described in Isaiah 11:1-9. He has the talent and ability to protect His bride. He always keeps His arms open for anyone and everyone to welcome them in His kingdom.

His body or the belly is like polished ivory which is decorated with lapis lazuli. Lapis lazuli is a stone. In some translations of the Bible instead of lapis lazuli the word "sapphire" is used. Sapphire also is a stone. Both lapis lazuli and sapphire have a blue color. The blue color is used in the tabernacle. In the tabernacle, it represents the "son of God". Sapphire was used in the breastplate of the priest (Exodus 28:18, 39:11), in the dress of Lucifer (Ezekiel 28:13), and the foundation of the holy city (Revelation 21:19). The elders of Israel saw Jesus. Under His feet, they saw sapphire. When Ezekiel saw Him, he saw sapphire/ lapis.

Ezekiel 10:1,

Then I looked, and see, in the expanse that was over the head of the cherubim there appeared above them as it were a sapphire.

Exodus 24:9-10,

Then Moses, Aaron, Nadab, Abihu, and seventy of the elders of Israel went up. They saw the God of Israel. Under his feet was like a paved work of sapphire stone, like the skies for clearness.

So the blue color in the form of thread in the tabernacle represents the son of God and the blue color in the form of stone represents the presence of God. The bride resembled His belly or body with polished ivory. Many ornaments and decoration pieces are made of bones of different animals but Ivory is the most expensive bone. In the past, it was used by rich people or kings in construction. Ivory is the tusk of an elephant. Whereas he is the strongest and powerful among all the animals. Some people associate the belly with emotions. The white color of ivory represents the positive and pure emotions of Jesus towards His bride. These emotions are strong. Polished ivory speaks about the smoothness or balance of these emotions. Love and anger both are emotions but when we go astray from Him, He doesn't consume us in His anger because He has polished or smooth emotions. He keeps His emotions balanced. He can keep them balanced because He has the presence of God in the form of blue colored stone. Now, this blue stone is fitted in ivory which looks as if the stone is a part of the ivory. It means Jesus has Godly emotions for His bride.

5:15

His legs are like pillars of marble set on sockets of fine gold. His appearance is like Lebanon, excellent as the cedars.

While talking about the beauty of the bridegroom, the bride said that His legs are pillars of marble. Marble is a beautiful and hard rock that comes in different colors. It is a hard rock that is used in construction work and in making different decorative items. Legs of marble show the beauty and firmness He has when He stands. The legs are like pillars. This shows the strength He has in His legs. Pillars are usually very strong. When we talk about pillars of marble, it means we are adding strength and beauty. He stands like an unshakeable pillar. His decisions are strong and when he decides something then no one can move Him. No one has the power to stop Him, question Him about His doings and no one can reverse His words. Numbers 23:19, "*God is not a man, that he should lie, nor a son of man, that he should repent. Has he said, and he won't do it? Or has he spoken, and he won't make it good?*"

His legs (pillars) are set on the bases of pure gold. In the tabernacle, most of the holy items were made of gold. Gold represents purity and divinity. Gold bases are like feet of Christ. As the legs of marble represent strong decisions and gold bases as feet to walk according to those decisions, it means Jesus' decisions are based on the Word of God (gold bases) and they are firm like marble pillars. In Song of Songs 5:11, the bride said that His head is the purest gold. Now she is saying His feet (bases) are of gold. The Head of a man thinks and His feet act according to those thoughts and fulfill the plans. It means His thoughts and actions are pure like gold. His thoughts are as pure as His actions. Sometimes we don't understand His thoughts and actions and because of our lack of education, we conclude the wrong meaning of His actions. Most of the time the Pharisees, scribes, and sometimes even His disciples didn't understand why He was doing the things He was doing. When he was talking to a woman on the well in Samaria, His disciples didn't understand why He was talking to a woman. Pharisees and scribes were not able to figure out why He was having fellowship with tax collectors and sinners. Sometimes we also don't understand His moves, but He is just in all His deeds.

The bride says that the appearance of the bridegroom is like a cedar from Lebanon. Cedar is a beautiful tall tree which is known for its strength in construction work. Cedars from Lebanon were considered the best. By comparing the bridegroom with cedar, she is saying that her beloved is a tall, strong, and handsome man. Cedar has a very unique characteristic. Its oil and shavings are used to keep the snakes and other reptiles away from the house. When Jesus is around us like a cedar, the old serpent (Lucifer) would not be able to harm us. We will be safe in His presence.

5:16

His mouth is sweetness; yes, he is altogether lovely. This is my beloved, and this is my friend, daughters of Jerusalem.

His mouth is sweetness means the words which come out of His mouth are worthy and acceptable. His word contains life. His word is life for individuals, nations, and the whole world. His word is not only valued on this earth but in heaven also. Angels wait for His word and move swiftly on the release of His word to fulfill the command. This is why we pray in the Lord's Prayer, *"Let your Kingdom come. Let your will be done on earth as it is in heaven."*(Matthew 6:10). Because, in heaven, His will is fulfilled as soon as He speaks.

After describing different attributes of His personality, the bride says that He is altogether lovely. The love is radiating out of Him. Every part of His body speaks about the unfailing love He has for us. Every part of His body was bruised and bleeds for us. He let His precious blood flow out of His body to write the story of love He had for us even before we were born and even before the creation of this world. Isaiah 53:2 says, *"For he grew up before him as a tender plant, and as a root out of dry ground. He has no good looks or majesty. When we see him, there is no beauty that we should desire him"*. He was beaten and bruised so badly that he was disfigured. He was disfigured to restore our spiritual beauty. His bruises may look ugly to non-believers but for believers, He shall be worshiped for the whole eternity for His bruises. Therefore He is altogether lovely for me and I am being his bride and child of God, altogether lovely for Him.

In Song of Songs 5:9, when the daughters of Jerusalem asked about her beloved, she started explaining about Jesus. She explained what He looks like from His head to toe. After finishing her explanation she said, *"This is my beloved"*. She painted a picture of her beloved by her words. What is the condition of the present-day bride? Are we ready to explain Jesus to others or we are hiding behind the bush? To explain about Him, we need to be close to Him. We need a personal experience of Him. John said that the Jesus we talk about is the Jesus we have personally experienced. Do we have a personal experience of Him or do we just talk about Him after hearing about Him from someone?

1-John 1:1

That which was from the beginning, that which we have heard, that which we have seen with our eyes, that which we saw, and our hands touched, concerning the Word of life.

6

6:1

Where has your beloved gone, you fairest among women? Where has your beloved turned, that we may seek him with you?

In Song of Songs chapter 5, we read how the bridegroom came to meet the bride. He had been knocking on the door but the bride took so long to open the door that He went away. Later she came out to look for Him. On the way, she found the daughters of Jerusalem. She explained to them what her beloved looks like. After learning about the appearance of the bridegroom, at the start of the 6th chapter, those women offered their help to find Him out. But they wanted some clue from her as to which direction they might find Him.

It is a spiritual law that if you are feeling spiritually depressed, then seek the fellowship of saints. The bride asked her friends who wanted to help her to seek the bridegroom. In the time of the earthly life of Jesus, there was a centurion. He asked some Jews to request Jesus to heal his servant, and Jesus accepted their request (Luke 7:1-5). In the same way, when different people intercede for someone, Jesus listens to them. In the case of the bride and bridegroom, friends wanted to help the bride to reach the bridegroom by standing in the gap between Jesus and the bride; so that bride could reach the bridegroom. This standing between the gaps is known as intercession.

When a church member feels being cut off from Christ, like the bride; other members need to intercede for him.

There are different types of people in this world. Some people think themselves more righteous than others. Such people were around Jesus when a lady who was not of good repute came to Jesus and anointed His head with a priced perfume. People started criticizing Jesus and that lady (Luke 7:36-39). The lady came from outside the self-righteous group, but from inside she was clean. The people who were inside the house were clean on the outside but filled with filth on the inside. Jesus doesn't like such people and calls them hypocrites. We can see another kind of group in Acts 10:22-48. This group consisted of Peter and a few Christians in Joppa. They went to the house of Cornelius and shared the Word of God. The gentiles there accepted Christ and became a part of the bride of Christ. We need friends and family members who can help us become one with Christ. The bride found such friends who offered their services to help the bride in searching for Christ with her.

6:2

My beloved has gone down to his garden, to the beds of spices, to pasture his flock in the gardens, and to gather lilies.

In Song of Songs, chapter 5, the bride was trying to find out the whereabouts of her beloved. The bride started her search for the bridegroom at night; she met the watchmen who misbehaved with her (Song of Songs 5:2-7). After that, she met with the daughters of Jerusalem. At that time of history, normally common people and especially women used to stay at home at night. The bride met the women in the street; as the bride met the women in the street, it means now it is the day. So she is searching for the bridegroom from night till morning. When her friends asked her, she described her beloved. After hearing the description the friends were ready to find the bridegroom. Instead of going around in search of the bridegroom, the bride said that she knows where He is. How did she come to know where He is? When her friends asked about her beloved, she started meditating about His personality. After meditating on Him in Song of Songs 5:10-16, she came to know that He will be in His garden. When we observe or study something or someone we get knowledge about him. When we meditate on that knowledge, we get revelation and revelations lead us into His presence. Joshua 1:8, "*This book of the law shall not depart from your mouth, but you shall meditate on it day and night, that you may observe to do according to all that is written in it; for then you shall make your way prosperous, and then you shall have good success.*" God didn't command only Joshua to meditate on His Word; this is valid for us as well. We all need success in our lives, relationships, health, spiritual life, and in the life after death. The secret of success is in meditation on His word.

Her beloved went to His garden where the beds of spices are. It means there are different spices in His garden. Spices are used for making medicines and perfumes. There are kinds of spices for different uses. God, Himself is our healer and there is healing in His Word (Exodus 15:26, Psalm 107:20). His Word acts like a spice for our physical and spiritual life. If we look at the Bible, we will find different books like different spices to maintain and heal our lives. For example, the Song of Songs is good to understand the relationship between husband and wife or between church and Christ. Prophetic books help us in understanding God's plan of salvation for nations. The book of Psalms helps us in understanding worship even in hard times. Ecclesiastes helps us in understanding the declining nature of this world and teaches us to live happily in whatever we have. Historic books in the Bible help us to know our heritage and Biblical roots of Christian culture. Different books of the Bible are different spices of God that are used for the healing of individuals and nations. This is the place where He feeds His flock and gathers the lilies.

The bride indicates that the bridegroom browses in the gardens to gather lilies. In the Bible, most of the places where you will find lilies, you will find King Solomon as well. In the temple, Solomon fashioned lily flowers on different things (1-Kings 7:19-26). In Luke 12:27 Jesus talked about lilies and He mentioned Solomon as well. It is interesting that lily flowers were not made on any utensil inside the temple but we can see them in the temple. We see lilies on the top of the pillars in the temple and on the rim of the water basin. When Jesus was ministering in the temple, the court of the gentiles was there. It was beside the main building of the temple. The court of the gentiles is not seen in the time of Solomon but in the second temple, which is also known as Herod's temple. King Herod extended the temple and added the court of the gentiles. Despite the addition of the court of the gentiles, Jesus didn't consider the temple as a less holy place. For Jesus, it was still holy, otherwise, why did He go there to worship from the days of His childhood. The pillars, on which the lily flowers appeared, and the basin, were not in the holy or holy of holies. They were in the courtyard. The court of the gentiles was next to the courtyard. In this way court of the gentiles and lilies seem connected with each other. When the bride says that He feeds His folks in His garden she is referring to the Israelites, and when He gathers lilies, this shows He is calling Gentiles to His kingdom.

6:3

I am my beloved's, and my beloved is mine. He browses among the lilies.

The same words the bride used in this verse were also used in Song of Songs 2:16. The repetition of the same words shows the confidence she has in her relationship with Christ. When she talks about the depth of relationship with Christ, she mentions that He browses among lilies. He feeds the people He cares for. He is the Shepherd of His people. We are his people, the sheep of his pasture (Psalm 100:3). He feeds them in green pastures. Psalm 23 is a wonderful description that how He feeds His sheep. The sheep in

His flock are not afraid even if they go through the valley of death. The presence of the Shepherd is enough to keep them safe. Even if an enemy encamps around us, we don't doubt his strength to shelter us. Our Shepherd feeds us without concern about the strength of the enemy. In ancient times, when the army of an enemy surrounded a city, the very first thing they do was cut off all the supply lines of the surrounded city. But Jesus is the bread of life and He is the water of life (John 4:5-14, 6:48). He is the way (John 14:6). No matter how mighty is our enemy, Jesus is mightier than him. If the enemy stops the food or water, we know that Jesus fills our cup to the brim. Satan can't block our way to prosperity because Jesus is the way where there is no way. He encourages us with the words, *"In the world you have trouble; but cheer up! I have overcome the world"* (John 16:33).

The bride has confidence in her relationship with the bridegroom. She says that she belongs to Him. We should be sure about our relationship. Jesus doesn't want a relationship in which someone else is involved with us. We can't have a deep relationship with Christ and with the world at the same time. Such relationships are not acknowledged by Jesus. This is why many people on the Day of Judgment will say that they had been serving Christ but Jesus will say that I don't have any relationship with you.

Matthew 7:21-23

"Not everyone who says to me, 'Lord, Lord,' will enter into the Kingdom of Heaven, but he who does the will of my Father who is in heaven. Many will tell me in that day, 'Lord, Lord, didn't we prophesy in your name, in your name cast out demons, and in your name do many mighty works?' Then I will tell them, 'I never knew you. Depart from me, you who work iniquity.'

Like good friends, our relationship should become deeper with the passage of time. When we look at the life of Daniel, he respected and obeyed God from the days of his youth. With the passage of time, his love and dedication kept on growing. When he was asking

God to reveal His secrets to him about the nation of Israel, he was quite old. In Daniel 10:11 and 10:19, the angel called him, *"Daniel, you greatly beloved man"*. We can also be Jesus' beloved, a highly esteemed person; if our relationship with Him becomes purer and purer.

6:4

You are beautiful, my love, as Tirzah, lovely as Jerusalem, awesome as an army with banners.

Tirzah was 60 Km away from Jerusalem. It was a beautiful city which became the capital city for some time (1-Kings 14:17, 15:21, 33, 16:8-23). The Bridegroom compared the beauty of the bride with Tirzah and Jerusalem. Jerusalem was a city chosen by God for His temple to be there. It was a city on the rock which was difficult to conquer (Lamentations 4:12).

Tirzah speaks about the physical beauty of the bride and Jerusalem speaks about the spiritual beauty and maturity of the bride. Both Tirzah and Jerusalem are the cities where kings had been living. It means we need to glorify God our king in both spiritual and physical ways. We are like a city and we need the king to be the head of the city (Proverbs 25:28). Our body and spirit should both be dedicated to God. Any lack of dedication in our spiritual or physical sphere is not liked by God. Daniel and his friends were loyal to God spiritually but their dedication was shown when they denied the food which was given by the King. They didn't want to defile themselves (Daniel 1:8). If they ate the food offered by the king, they would be defiling their bodies because some Bible teachers say that the food was first offered to an idol and then anyone else was allowed to take it. Stephen's spirit was already safe but he offered his body as a sacrifice by bearing the strikes of stones on his body when people were stoning him. Even in that agony, he was praising God (Acts 7:59). He glorified God not only in his spirit but also in his body. When we offer our body and spirit to God almighty then we become beautiful like Tirzah and Jerusalem.

The bride looks as majestic as troops marching with banners. There are two kinds of troops, one with banners and others without a banner. When troops come out with a King, or with the permission of the king, they have their banner with them. When troops enter some territory illegally, they tried to hide their identity. Satan and sin are the ones who try to enter without any banner or identification. When Satan entered Eden, he hid in the serpent. When Cain was angry with his brother, God told him that sin is hiding and wanted to enter in Cain's heart (Genesis 4:7). Whenever we go out, we should carry His banner with us. When people come into contact with us, they may feel the difference we have in our lives (Acts 4:13). They may say that *"God is among you indeed"* (1-Corinthians 14:24-25). They will see the banner of God on us.

6:5

Turn away your eyes from me, for they have overcome me. Your hair is like a flock of goats, that lie along the side of Gilead.

When two people like each other, they love to see each other. Once I was with my friends. There was a lady among us. After some time her husband came in, and as soon as she saw her husband a glow was seen in her eyes. Although we all were good friends the love she had for her husband was speaking loudly through her eyes. People who understand each other can communicate through their eyes.

When the bride looked at the bridegroom, she communicated the love she had for Him through her eyes. These love thoughts touched the emotions of the bridegroom. When someone truly loves a person, they often think about that person. Sometimes these thoughts ignite a fire in us.

Psalm 39:3,

"My heart was hot within me. While I meditated, the fire burned. I spoke with my tongue."

In Psalm 45:1 psalmist says, *"My heart overflows with a noble theme. I recite my verses for the king. My tongue is like the pen of a skillful writer."*

According to the psalmist, some thoughts about the beauty of God came into his heart. He kept on thinking about them. Those thoughts took the form of a song. He opened his mouth and used his tongue to speak out those praises. This whole process started with thoughts. Those thoughts controlled the mind and he used his tongue to praise God. God can read and understand our thoughts. Many times He read the thoughts of Pharisees which were against Him. In Luke 7:36-50, we see two main characters. The first one was the Pharisee who invited Jesus to a meal. The second one was a lady who poured out expensive perfume on the head of Jesus. The Pharisee thought poorly of Jesus and Jesus knew his thoughts. On the other hand, the lady was thinking about the sins she committed and about the mercy of Jesus. Neither the Pharisee nor the lady spoke any word from their mouth but Jesus knew what was in their hearts. Similarly, when we think about Jesus, His cross, love, mercy, and sacrifice, overwhelm us.

The bridegroom talks about the hair of the bride. Her hair looks like a flock which is descending from Gilead. Although a woman's hair is part of her beauty, the Bible says hair is for her covering (1-Corinthians 11:15). To cover something means to separate that thing. We need to separate ourselves unto God. This separation will keep us attached to God. The more we are attached to God, the more blessing of God will flow through us to the world. The hairs don't cover a person/ lady fully. It means we are not required to totally stay away from the world. We need to stay in the world but we are not of the world. Paul explains this fact in 1-Corinthians 5:9-11, *"I wrote to you in my letter to have no company with sexual sinners; yet not at all meaning with the sexual sinners of this world, or with the covetous and extortionists, or with idolaters; for then you would have to leave the world. But as it is, I wrote to you not to associate with anyone who is called a brother who is a sexual sinner, or covetous, or an idolater, or a slanderer, or a drunkard, or an extortionist. Don't even eat with such a person".*

The bridegroom says that your hair is like goats on the hills. Leviticus 4:23-28, tells that goats were being used for the sin offering. Thoughts and hairs both come out of our heads. By praising the hairs, the bridegroom is praising the thoughts the bride has. When goats come down from a hill, from far they look like someone is producing a wavy pattern. It means your hair flows in waves. But those goats are coming from the hills of Gilead. Gilead was the place that was well known for the production of balm (Jeremiah 8:22, 46:11). Balm was used as a medicine for healing wounds. In other words, Jesus is saying that you have the ointment to heal the nation. Hair as the beauty of the bride and Gilead as a place of ointment means the beauty of the bride is related to the provision of healing for the nations. We, as Christ's representative, need to present the power Jesus has to heal the physical and spiritual wounds of the individuals and nations in this world.

6:6

Your teeth are like a flock of ewes, which have come up from the washing, of which every one has twins; not one is bereaved among them.

While describing the beauty of the bride, the bridegroom talks about the teeth of the bride and He compares them with the sheep which have twins. This shows the health of sheep is quite good. It means the bride's teeth are healthy and beautiful.

Teeth are used for holding and crushing the food. If we don't chew the food correctly, our digestive system will either have to work more or our stomach will become upset. It means teeth are responsible for taking care of what is going inside our body. The bride should take care of the teaching or information which is coming into the church. God appointed different people in the church to monitor the activities and teachings which are being shared from the pulpit. The Apostle Paul taught us that when anyone speaks prophecy in the church, people should listen and weigh carefully that the speaker is speaking the truth from God or not. It is not only applicable to prophecies; we should take care of the sermons also which are being preached in the church.1-Corinthians 14:29, *"Let the prophets speak, two or three, and let the others discern."*

In Matthew 15:1-11, Jesus corrected Pharisees and their followers about the teachings on respecting parents. Although the Pharisees were offended by the teachings of Jesus, this bitter pill was necessary for the health of the nation. People were accepting the wrong teachings of the Pharisees as the truth. The bride should have healthy teeth to take the right things in them and the right teachings they get, they should chew them properly. So, they can digest the Word and properly benefit from the Word of God.

6:7

Your temples are like a piece of a pomegranate behind your veil.

Temples are a very sensitive part of our body. Any injury to the temple can be fatal. In Judges 4:21, Jael hammered a tent peg through the temple of Sisera and he died in the camp. The temple is the juncture where four skull bones meet together. It helps in chewing. The temporal lobes play an important role in processing emotions and language.

The bridegroom compared the bride's temples with pomegranates. The pomegranate is an important fruit of Israel since ancient times (Deuteronomy 8:8). Pomegranates of gold were used to decorate the hem of the high priest's robe (Exodus 28:34, 39:26). When spies went to Canaan, they brought three fruits back from there; one of the fruit was pomegranate (Numbers 13:23). According to some traditions in Israel, some people relate the six spikes on the top of the pomegranate, which forms the shape of the crown, with the Star of David. If you join those spikes on the top of the pomegranate by drawing a line, you will get the shape of the Star of David.

People in Israel value pomegranate a lot in their country because it is not only good for health but it reveals some other things as well. Some people say that if you count the seeds inside a pomegranate, they will be 613. There are 613 laws taught by Moses in the Bible. Each Bible verse is the Word of God that has life in it. Similarly, every seed in the pomegranate has life in it. It reproduces itself in the form of a tree after being sown in the ground. In Matthew 13, Jesus represented the Word of God by a seed which produces life.

The two huge pillars Solomon made in the temple were named Boaz and Jakin. He fashioned pomegranates near the top of the pillars (2-Chronicles 3:16-17). The meaning of Boaz is "He strengthens" and the meaning of Jakin is "He establishes". In between these two pillars, there was a beautiful door to enter the main building of the Solomon temple; its name was "Way". The other two doors which lead to the Holy and Holy of Holies were named "Truth" and "life" respectively. Jesus said, "*I am the way, the truth, and the life. No one comes to the Father, except through me*" (John 14:6). By this statement, Jesus meant that only through me, you can enter into the presence of God. Imagine if you will, that two pillars are in the temple and in between them there is a door. The door, which is Jesus Christ, is saying that if you want to be established (Boaz) with strength (Jakin), come to me. But how you will receive that strength? Look at the top of the pillars, you will find pomegranates which represent the Word of God. So you will be established by the Word of God through Jesus.

The bridegroom looked at the bride and said that "*Your temples are like a piece of a pomegranate*". Temples are attached to the brain and control emotions and language. Pomegranates are representing the

Word of God. By combining these facts we can say that bridegroom is saying that your language and emotions are according to the Word of God. Words explain our emotions. If our emotions are right, our words will be right as well.

1-Peter 4:11, *"If anyone speaks, let it be as it were the very words of God."*

6:8

There are sixty queens, eighty concubines, and virgins without number.

In Hebrew, every alphabet letter is associated with a number. Therefore sometimes Bible teachers use numbers to understand the meanings of verses. In the case of verse 8, we will try to understand one aspect of the verse through numbers. Sixty and eighty are both multiples of ten. Ten multiply by six is sixty, and eight multiply by ten is eighty. Six is the number of a man; on the 6th day, the man was made. Eight is the number of new beginnings and ten is the number of favor and responsibility. Obeying the Ten Commandments was the responsibility of the Israelites. Abraham's servant went with ten camels and with the best gifts from his master with a responsibility to find a woman to marry Isaac (Genesis 24:10). Rebecca's parents asked for the favor for ten days that their daughter may stay with them before she could go to Isaac (Genesis 24:55). Joseph sent ten asses and ten she-asses with food and gifts to his father to show the favor and respect he had for his father (Genesis 45:23). So we see that number ten is mostly associated with responsibility and favor.

The Bridegroom compared His beloved with two groups of women sixty queens and eighty concubines. Queens are the elite class and concubines were considered as lower-class women. Normally wives were taken from Israelite women and concubines were gentiles but it was not a hard and fast rule. Queens are representing Israelites. Queens are representing Israelites. When He compared her with sixty queens, it means she is more beautiful as compared to any other woman near Him. Figuratively eighty concubines are the people from gentiles who are starting their new journey with Christ. We may say that concubines were not considered equal to wives but when we study the Bible, we will find that God gave the concubines the same rights as wives. His bride represents the people who truly identify with Christ. In this way, His bride becomes more beautiful than anyone, whether they are from the Israelites or gentiles.

The third group with which Jesus compared His bride is "virgins". Virgins are the women who are not in a marital relationship with anyone. There are people in this world who clearly say that they belong to Christ. Other people will say that they belong to some other god. There is another group that says that they are not associated with any god and called themselves atheists. Anyone who is not associated with God associates himself with Satan because the one who doesn't have His Spirit doesn't belong to God. So the people who associate themselves with other gods, and the people who don't associate themselves with any god, both belong to Satan because according to the Bible there is no middle ground. You will belong to Christ or Satan. Therefore His bride is the best lady in the world because she clearly proclaims that I belong to my beloved and my beloved belongs to me (Song of Songs 6:3).

6:9

My dove, my perfect one, is unique. She is her mother's only daughter. She is the favorite one of her who bore her. The daughters saw her, and called her blessed. The queens and the concubines saw her, and they praised her.

The dove is considered a clean bird. The dove was used as an offering on the altar. Usually, it was used as a sacrifice in the case of healing from leprosy. A dove was an option for poor people to sacrifice instead of other expensive animals. By comparing the bride with a dove, the bridegroom says that His bride is holy, peaceful, and clean as a dove. She is ready to go into the world and help the people to come out of spiritual leprosy, which is sin. She is ready to be sacrificed. In many countries, Christians are hated and burnt alive. His bride is being tortured but she is ready to march forward.

His bride is the perfect one and unique. This is not the perfection that we can get on our own. People in the world try to make their relationship perfect with their god through good works. But our good works are not good enough to make a place for us in heaven. Therefore Jesus did all the work. He finished that work on the cross and said, *"It is finished"*. We rely on His finished work on the cross for our perfection, not on our own works. He perfected Israel with His glory (Ezekiel 16:14). Because of the perfection, He gave us, we became unique. No one else in this world has the perfection we have. We are perfected by His blood and glory. No other nation can have this perfection because His blood and glory are only available to His people.

The bridegroom speaks about the reasons that make His bride unique. She is the only daughter of her mother and her mother loves her a lot. A church is like a mother to new believers. When someone accepts the Lord and comes into the church, the church needs to welcome him. Sometimes when people don't see acceptance in church people, they become offended, go astray, and join some other group. Our God loves us. He loves each one of us as His only child. His love for us as a group or individual is the same.

Women saw the bride and praised her. Most of the time women represent nations in the Bible. So other nations saw Israel and blessed it (Genesis 18:18, Isaiah 61:9, Malachi 3:12). Abraham was blessed by God. His blessings were seen by the king and he admitted that God is with him (Genesis 21:22-24). Jacob and his uncle had a covenant because God blessed Jacob (Genesis 31:43-48). King Balak saw blessed Israel and became afraid (Numbers 22:1-6). In the time of King David and King Solomon, the blessings on Israel were well known in different parts of the world (1-Kings 4:34). When we walk truly and uprightly with our God, then people and nations praise us.

6:10

Who is she who looks out as the morning, beautiful as the moon, clear as the sun, and awesome as an army with banners?

The writer of Hebrews in chapter 11 gives the definition of faith as, *"Now faith is assurance of things hoped for, proof of things not seen."* The friends are asking the bride about the one who will surely come. They are very much assured that He will come. This surety is known as faith. The bride, and friends of the bride, are waiting for the bridegroom. The bride all over the world is waiting for the coming of Jesus Christ. He promised us that He will come to take us home with him. It is a test for us that we may not lose our hope and don't sleep spiritually (Matthew 25:1-13). Like a watchman, we need to be awakened (Revelation 16:15) so that no one can take away our clothes.

The bridegroom is compared with the moon and sun. He is cool as the moon and necessary as the sun. When He shows His humanity, He is cool as the moon but when He shows His divinity, He is brighter than the sun (Revelation 1:16, 10:1).

There are many references in the Bible where God and Jesus were called the sun. In Psalm 84:11 God is called the sun. In Luke 1:78, Jesus is described as a rising sun. In Bible God is called the sun; His son Jesus is called the sun and we, who are adopted sons (Ephesians 1:5) are also called the sun.

Matthew 13:43, *"Then the righteous will shine like the sun in the Kingdom of their Father."*

When the bridegroom will come, that will be a time of immense joy. His people will be happy because He will remove their pains and tears. When Jesus came on earth, he came healing the sick. Wherever He went, people gathered around Him and women were blessing the lady who got the chance to raise Him since His childhood. A woman in the crowd said, *"Blessed is the womb that bore you, and the breasts which nursed you!"* (Luke 11:27). When He will come back, He will come as God. At some places in the Old and New Testaments, Jesus had been appearing in His radiant glory. When He will next come, He will come with His angels. When Jesus and His angels come in glory, it will be beyond the capacity of any human to bear that glory. Daniel 12:3 says, *"Those who are wise will shine as the brightness of the expanse. Those who turn many to righteousness will shine as the stars forever and ever".* We see that believers are represented as stars and Jesus is represented as sun. We are the stars who need Jesus as the sun to be illuminated. Therefore Jesus is prominent among all.

6:11

I went down into the nut tree grove, to see the green plants of the valley, to see whether the vine budded, and the pomegranates were in flower.

The Bridegroom went to the orchard and he wanted to inspect the growth. He inspected the growth on the nut trees. He also looked at the small plants in the valley. Small plants are the new believers and children of believers. He cares for the children as well. They are so important in the kingdom of God that God appointed an angel for each child (Matthew 18:10) and Paul taught that the children of believers are considered holy in God's kingdom (1-Corinthians 7:14). It is necessary that we keep on praying for the children because they are the prime target of Satan. If he would be able to spoil our children, he would be spoiling the church of tomorrow. He always tries to sow the bitter seeds when the crop is still in its early phase (Matthew 13:24-30). We need to take care and be awake spiritually because the enemy came when people were sleeping and sowed the wrong kind of seed. This wrong kind of seed can be false teachings people are trying to teach in different places to kids that there is no

God; or that there is no harm if we speak lies for a good cause and other thoughts which are against Bible. If we are not vigilant enough about our kids, we can lose them spiritually. A very good example can be seen in Isaiah.

Isaiah 46:3-4

Listen to me, house of Jacob, and all the remnant of the house of Israel, that have been carried from their birth, that have been carried from the womb. Even to old age I am he, and even to gray hairs I will carry you. I have made, and I will bear. Yes, I will carry, and will deliver.

God said that He carried the Israelites since their birth. He has the ability to carry and sustain them in their old age and He will take care of them till the end. Notice that God is not leaving them at any stage. We will never be mature enough to stay away from our spiritual father. No matter how mature we are, if God will leave us we will not be able to sustain our spiritual life. In the same way, we need to take care of our children spiritually.

Jesus is not only concerned with the little ones. He knows that He needs to look after the spiritually mature as well. The bridegroom went and inspected the nut trees. Nuts are the fruit and fruit can be seen on the trees when they are mature. Almost all the nuts have oil in them and they are covered with some hard covering. The trees in His garden are the people who have spiritual oil in them which represents anointing. Believers also have a hard covering of protection of the blood of Christ.

Jesus as our bridegroom looks at the flowers of vines and pomegranates. In John 15:5 Jesus said, *"I am the vine. You are the branches"*. Jesus compared believers with branches. He came into the orchard and inspected the branches to check if the flowers are blooming on them or not. After the flower, the next stage is the fruit. The fruit is necessary for the lives of believers because it gives glory to God (John 15:8). He inspects pomegranate trees as well. He wanted to see flowers on them. We already discussed in Song of Songs 6:7 that pomegranates represent the Word of God. The believers (vine) and the Word (pomegranate) are closely associated with each other. By searching for flowers in the vine and the pomegranates, Jesus is saying that He wants to see a constant growth in believers.

6:12

Without realizing it, my desire set me with my royal people's chariots.

In the previous verse, we saw that it is the desire of Jesus Christ to see fruit in believers. He went to the orchard to see the flowers in vine and pomegranates. The words in this verse show that the bridegroom was not on the real chariot. The bridegroom felt himself on the chariots of His people. Chariots were used by royal people. By studying Bible, we see a pattern among the kings that they used to appoint their own sons and daughters on high ranking posts. In the same way, God is the King and His people are His children. He considers them high ranking officers. Officers have the authority and His people have the authority given by their heavenly father. So the people we see who have the royal chariots are the believers. The king is not using His own chariot. He is using the chariot of His people. By seeing the growth and work of His people, the king is so much fascinated that He feels himself in a fast moving chariot in His thoughts. Chariots in this situation show the strength and swiftness of the bridegroom's imagination. It was a kind of imaginary situation in which He is moving very fast in His thoughts. He was in His orchard examining the trees and plants there. His desire was to see his orchard's growth. This desire took Him in the next phase where he thought about the well-being of His orchard or the people of His kingdom. When He sees flowers or growth in His people, He desires to bless us further.

Jeremiah 29:11

For I know the thoughts that I think toward you," says Yahweh, "thoughts of peace, and not of evil, to give you hope and a future.

We don't need to live our lives according to our thoughts and plans. We need to take His plans. Our plans can fail but His plans can never be foiled. In the days of a Covid-19 pandemic, many people in different parts of the world have committed suicide. The usual cause of suicide is that people see failure in their lives. This failure could be the failure to fulfill the plans they made. Instead of thinking about fulfilling our plans, we need to see God and His plans. Our plans can be foiled but His plans can never be foiled. When His plans become our plans, then our plans will also not fail and we will be safe from disappointment and suicide.

When God called Abraham, God was not only thinking to bless him in his present situation. His thoughts were to bless him until the end of the world. It was not only for Abraham, every believer is precious in God's sight and He doesn't only have the plans to bless them in this world but also in the world to come. This fact was explained by Apostle Paul in 1-Corinthians 15:19, "*If we have only hoped in Christ in this life, we are of all men most pitiable*". Abraham and believers throughout the world, by accepting God as their supreme ruler, allow God's plans and desires to activate in their lives. When we accept God's call for repentance, salvation, obedience, submission, and fruitfulness; He starts thinking of blessing us even more abundantly. When He saw the growth in His orchard, His desire to do more for His orchard/ people took Him swiftly to a world where He was seeing His people blooming with their full strength.

6:13

Return, return, Shulammite! Return, return, that we may gaze at you. Why do you desire to gaze at the Shulammite, as at the dance of Mahanaim?

Shulammite was the lady Solomon loved. In Song of Songs, she represents the church. Both bride and bridegroom wanted to be with each other. The bride's heart is beating for her beloved. She wanted to go to Him but her friends are calling her. They want that the bride should stay with them. There are times in our lives when we know in our hearts that this is our prayer time, but we prefer the company of our friends and we deal with Jesus as a second-class citizen.

There are always such times when we need to make a decision. A time came in the life of Joseph when Potiphar's wife wanted Joseph to be with her but he ran away from there. We shouldn't stay at the places where we are being tempted to commit sin. We need to run from sins (1-Corinthians 6:18). Giving preference to our work or friends more than Jesus is a sin (Matthew 10:37).

Jesus took Judas Iscariot from this world and honored him as one of His disciples. While he was faithful, he was serving and healing the people throughout Israel (Matthew 10:1-10). A time came when the desires of this world started calling him. He started looking back to them by stealing the offerings and going to the chief priests to betray Jesus (Matthew 26:14-16). As a result, he lost his position as a disciple, physical life, and spiritual life (Acts 1:15-22). We shouldn't go back to this world if it calls us. The bride kept on going towards her beloved, ignoring all the voices which were trying to hold her back. Spiritual life is like a race in which we are running in a stadium. The people in the arena buck up the athletes with their claps and cheers. If an athlete stops and starts looking at the people in the arena, he will lose the race. The bride is running a spiritual race; friends are calling her from behind. These friends are the similitude of the attractions of this world which tries to grab our attention and we need to avoid such distractions.

When friends were calling the bride and she was not answering them because she didn't want any kind of diversion, the bridegroom answered them in the form of a question that "Why do you desire to gaze at the Shulammite?" It is the style of Jesus that sometimes He answers people in the form of a question. It is a good way to answer because it encourages people to think more and explore to find the answer. He often asked questions of His opponents in response to their questions.

The Bridegroom put the question, "Why would you gaze on the Shulammite as on the dance of Mahanaim? In some translations instead of "Mahanaim", the word "two armies" is used. The Word Mahanaim was first used in Genesis 32:1-2. Mahanaim means God's army or God's hosts. The bridegroom is asking, "Is the Shulammite, a dance of God's army"? In ancient times, if an army was defeated, the soldiers entered the city, hiding their faces. The winning army, while entering in their country or city used to dance. Being God's people, we are God's hosts. When we do not listen to the world, we will enter heavenly Jerusalem in a victorious way. The angels and all the heavenly creatures will welcome us with the sound of trumpets (1-Corinthians 15:51-55).

We shouldn't behave like a dance of two different armies. If both the armies are dancing, it means they are on the battleground and they are showing their war dance to show their strength or skill to the opponent to dominate them mentally. If we are living a godly life, then at some moment we hear the voice of Satan, and we incline our ear to listen to him, then we are dancing to his beat. We need to decide whose army we belong to. We shouldn't be dancing the dance of two armies. We need to move to the beat of Jesus' army.

7

7:1

How beautiful are your feet in sandals, prince's daughter! Your rounded thighs are like jewels, the work of the hands of a skillful workman.

In Exodus 3:5, God asked Moses to take off his shoes, but in Luke 15:22, the father asked His servants to give shoes to His son. Moses was living a life for his own self. He was trying to save himself from Pharaoh, but God wanted him to be a savior for many. In order to show how wrong he was, God showed him that he needs to leave his previous life behind like the dirty shoes he was wearing. In the case of the prodigal son, he had lost everything. The shoes which took him away from his father were bad habits. Those shoes were now broken. Now he was without shoes. The Father gave him a new pair of shoes because now he thought to walk on the path suggested by the father.

In Exodus 12:11, God told Moses that while eating Passover they should keep their sandals on. Putting on sandals shows the readiness of a person to do something. The sandals on the bride's feet show that she is ready to obey the commands of the bridegroom. When someone is dying or going on a journey from where it is uncertain when he will be back, then he gives advice to the people who will be taking care of the things after him. When Jesus went to His father after completing His mission on this earth, He opened His heart to His disciples and told them His desire. His desire is revealed in Matthew 28:16-20. The main emphasis of this talk can be seen in the words, *"go and make disciples of all nations"*. The bride has put on the sandals to fulfill the desire of the bridegroom to go to the nations and make disciples. Whereas Christ as our bridegroom will remain with us till the end of this earth; *"I am with you always, even to the end of the age"*

The bridegroom talked about the beauty of the legs of the bride. The legs of the bride are as beautiful as jewels. People use different exercises to make their legs a beautiful shape. Leg muscles are built up by walking. The prominence of the bride's legs shows that she had been working hard to spread the gospel. The legs are so beautiful they are praised as the work of an artist's hand. The artist who made the legs is Christ. If we think that we can do the work without Christ, then it will be a failure. Our success is with Christ. Without Christ, our works will be religion, not spirituality. In Christianity, there is no place for religion because Christianity is not a religion. It is a relationship with Christ. No matter how hard we are working, Christ should be the center of everything we do. If our own self is the center of our work, then it is not acceptable in God's kingdom, and on the Day of Judgment Jesus will simply say that He doesn't know us. The shape of our legs only becomes beautiful when we allow Jesus to take charge and shape them. Once disciples wanted to preach at a place named "Mysia" but Jesus told them through His spirit that they shouldn't preach in that area (Acts 16:7). Like disciples, we need to understand God's guidance about ministry. When we walk according to His guidance, our legs will become more and more beautiful because then they will be shaped by Christ.

7:2

Your body is like a round goblet, no mixed wine is wanting. Your waist is like a heap of wheat, set about with lilies.

The navel is an important part of our body. Before birth, a child takes food from his mother through the navel. It is the center of gravity of the human body. As a child takes its food from its mother, so we need to take our spiritual food from God. He gives us spiritual food in the form of His word. In Proverbs, Solomon said that the fear of the Lord is the health of our body and bones. In some translations instead of "body", the word "navel" is used.

Proverbs 3:7-8, *"Don't be wise in your own eyes. Fear Yahweh, and depart from evil. It will be health to your body, and nourishment to your bones."* The key to the health of the navel/ body is the fear of the Lord; but how we can have the fear of the Lord? The key is given in Deuteronomy. Deuteronomy 31:12, *"Assemble the people, the men and the women and the little ones, and the foreigners who are within your gates, that they may hear, learn, fear Yahweh your God, and observe to do all the words of this law."*

The key to the fear of the Lord is listening to the Word of God. From the above two verses, we conclude that the fear of the Lord is necessary for the health of our body and this fear is gained by listening to the Word. The navel is like a goblet that is filled with fine wine. When Jesus was having His last supper with His disciples, He represented His blood with wine (Matthew 26:26-27). So the navel which is the source of our first food is filled with the blood of Christ. It means that right from the very beginning a believer needs Christ's blood for his growth. That blood will never lose its strength and the quantity of blood will be enough for anyone. The blood of Christ is the best wine we could ever have. It is the center-point of the Christian life as the navel is the center of the body.

The waist of the bride is like a heap of wheat. Wheat is a blessing of God for His people. When God promised Canaan to the Israelites,

He said that it is a land of wheat (Deuteronomy 8:8). Wheat was used as an offering to God (1-Chronicles 21:23). Wheat is a blessing for men and an offering to God. The waist being called a heap of wheat means that people will get their spiritual food from the church. Food is necessary for the growth and continuity of life. It means the church should lead the world to prosperity. People in the church are the people who have a true relationship with Jesus. Such people have a life that they can share with the world. John 7:38 says, *"He who believes in me, as the Scripture has said, from within him will flow rivers of living water."* For the world around us, the church has food and water. Therefore the church is a blessing for the world.

7:3

Your two breasts are like two fawns, that are twins of a roe.

Fawns are young deer in the first year of their life. The average lifespan of a gazelle is 12 to 15 years. By saying that your breasts are like fawns, means they have a long lifespan ahead of them. Gazelle run very fast for long distances and they live together in herds. Jesus is saying that my bride has a long race to run. It is a race against time to save people from Satan and sin. The breasts' main purpose in the body is to feed the young. So the bridegroom is saying to the bride that you have to feed my young ones for a long time. For two thousand years, the bride has been raising the children, feeding them, and sending them into the world with a message of hope and reconciliation with God.

In Genesis 24:60 Rebecca was blessed by her family as, *"Our sister, may you be the mother of thousands of ten thousands, and let your offspring possess the gate of those who hate them"*. Rebecca's family knew that as she is going to be married, she will become a wife and then a mother. They prayed for her children that they may possess the cities of their enemies. This prayer was fulfilled when the Israelites occupied Canaan. This prayer is still being fulfilled now that Israelites are coming back and occupying their former territory. Rebecca was the mother of Jacob who was called Israel. The church is known as spiritual Israel. The blessing of Rebecca is working in spiritual Israel also, because every day we are defeating our spiritual enemy and occupying his territory. When we win a soul for Christ that means we have occupied a city in which our enemy was ruling. A new soul is a child in Christ who needs spiritual nourishment. This nourishment is given by the church with spiritual milk through spiritual breasts.

7:4

Your neck is like an ivory tower. Your eyes are like the pools in Heshbon by the gate of Bathrabbim. Your nose is like the tower of Lebanon which looks toward Damascus.

Ivory was an expensive commodity. Towers were necessary from a military point of view. These days an army uses radar and satellites to track the movement of the enemy but in ancient times, towers were in use. The neck is a sensitive part of the body. Our body needs a neck for the continuity of our breath. In ancient times and even now in some parts of the world, people carry out capital punishment by cutting through the neck. So our neck is a lifeline to us. Through our neck, sounds are produced. We can divide the sounds into two types. One type of sound is for God, which may include our prayers, intercession, praise, worship, or any conversation which is between us and God. The other kind of sound is the sound that we produce for the people around us, to communicate with them.

Comparing the neck with an ivory tower shows that there are warnings that are coming through that neck and they are precious to know. These warnings are not for God because God knows everything beforehand and we can't warn God. There is nothing in this world that can surprise God. Nothing can take God by surprise. So these warnings are for the people. Personally, we can't see in the spirit world to warn anyone. Therefore God has given us some ministry tools which are known as "gifts of Spirit." Out of nine spiritual gifts mentioned in 1-Corinthians 12:4-11, three are known as "vocal gifts". These gifts are "prophecy, different kinds of tongues, and interpretation of tongues." When these gifts are used in church then the church will be warning believers about different dangers which are coming in personal lives, other's lives, and the dangers which are coming in the world. For example, Nathan the prophet talked with David about the problem in his personal life (2-Samuel 12:1-12). In Acts 11:28, a prophet named Agabus warned the church that there will be a severe famine in the Roman world. God has given us a huge pile of information in the Bible; which is valid for all the times but sometimes God gives us some other information through His church. When the church declares this information, God appreciates this act of faith and says your neck is like an ivory tower.

The bridegroom compared the eyes of the bride with pools of Heshbon. Bath Rabbim means "daughter of many." Heshbon was a city captured by Israelites from Canaanites.

Numbers 21:25-26

Israel took all these cities. Israel lived in all the cities of the Amorites, in Heshbon, and in all its villages. For Heshbon was the city of Sihon the king of the Amorites, who had fought against the former king of Moab, and taken all his land out of his hand, even to the Arnon.

The bridegroom compared the bride's neck with a tower. This tower is to proclaim the news which is received by God. Water sources were the lifeline of any city. Most of the ancient settlements were near the rivers or springs. Bath Rabbim was one of the city gates of Heshbon. When God tells us something, it is not only to announce like an announcement from a tower. It must have some effect on our own lives as well. When the Israelites were leaving Egypt, they made a golden calf and worshiped it. God became angry and told Moses about this. God was so angry that he wanted to kill all of them. Moses started interceding for the Israelites (Exodus chapter 32). When God was angry with King Saul, Samuel was interceding and weeping before God (1-Samuel 16:1). Abraham interceded for Sodom (Genesis 18:20-33). The tears which come out of our eyes to intercede for God's people are like water from the pools of Heshbon and our eyes are like those pools.

Jeremiah the prophet is known as the weeping prophet. He had been weeping before God for his people.

Jeremiah 9:1, *"Oh that my head were waters, and my eyes a spring of tears, that I might weep day and night for the slain of the daughter of my people!"*

Lamentations 2:18, *"Their heart cried to the Lord. O wall of the daughter of Zion, let tears run down like a river day and night. Give yourself no relief. Don't let your eyes rest."*

Next, the bridegroom talked about the nose of the bride. The bride's nose is like a tower of Lebanon which is looking towards Damascus. Towers are usually very high to monitor and target the moves of the enemy. A high nose like a tower is considered a sign of beauty in some cultures. The nose is used to smell different things. In this verse, the bridegroom is pointing out and praising the ability of the bride to smell the danger. Sometimes we are deceived by our eyes but when we smell something, we smell it even without seeing it. In Judges 9:31-41, we read about Gaal and Zebul. Zebul saw the troops coming to attack the city but he confused them with the shadow of mountains. The troops attacked and killed many in the city. So sometimes we are mistaken by our natural senses. But to judge spiritual matters God has given His people a supernatural ability to sense the smell of danger. Paul the apostle sensed the danger in one of the journeys (Acts 27:9-44).

Acts 27:10, *"Sirs, I perceive that the voyage will be with injury and much loss, not only of the cargo and the ship, but also of our lives."*

Acts 27: 41*"But coming to a place where two seas met, they ran the* *vessel aground. The bow struck and remained immovable, but the stern began to break up by the violence of the waves."*

In Acts 27:10, Paul didn't say that "God told me" or "I have seen a vision" or "an angel told me", instead of all these things he smelled the upcoming danger in his spirit. What he said was true and we see that when the officer didn't listen to him, they lost the ship. We need to ask God to give us a good sense of spiritual smell.

The nose is a tower which is in Lebanon and looking towards Damascus. Damascus is an ancient city; its name is mentioned in the story of Abraham (Genesis 14:15). Lebanon was a very beautiful place under Israelite control. Damascus was the place where the enemy was living and they have their garrison over there. Several times, enemies attacked from Damascus (2-Samuel 8:5, 1-Kings 15:18). In Amos 1:3-5, God declared that Damascus would be punished for its deeds. The bride's nose should be sensitive to detect the motion of the spiritual enemies around her.

7:5

Your head on you is like Carmel. The hair of your head like purple. The king is held captive in its tresses.

Carmel was a city in Israel. This was the city where Saul erected a monument in his own honor (1-Samuel 15:12). David had been hiding from Saul in this area; his wife was from the same area as well (1-Samuel 27:3, 25:39). Mount Carmel was the place where Elijah and the prophets of Baal had a contest. Elijah won the contest and killed the prophets of Baal. This is the same mountain where Elijah prayed to God for the rain in Israel (1-Kings 18:16-46). Elisha had been living in the same area (2-Kings 4:25). So Carmel is the place of attraction to royal people and men of God; a place of the people who lead revivals.

When Jesus our bridegroom says that your head is like Carmel, it means your thoughts are the thoughts of royal people and men of God. In other words, your thoughts are the thoughts of a man of God who is the king as well. Such a man will think two kinds of thoughts; first to increase his kingdom and secondly about the prosperity of his people. Being a church we need to expand God's kingdom and think about the prosperity of God's people. If we think of such thoughts and do our best to implement them under God's guidance, then we will be known as true worshipers of God.

Regarding the bride's hair, the bridegroom says that it is like a tapestry. A tapestry is a fine woven work. As it is a royal tapestry, so the color most probably was purple. So the hairs are like purple threads which are designed beautifully, like a tapestry. At first, the bridegroom talked about the head, and then he talked about the hair. The thoughts in the head can't be seen outwardly. But purple hair shows that the bride is not only having kingly thoughts inwardly, she also looks like a king's bride outwardly. When our thoughts are for God's kingdom and our actions match our thoughts, then our actions would be visible like purple threads or like women's hair. King David's thoughts were to build a temple for God (1-Chronicles 17:1-2). Those thoughts were beautiful and high like Mount Carmel. He started gathering the materials to build the temple (1-Chronicles chapter 22). Those actions are still visible to people in the Bible. Those actions are like purple hairs that catch everyone's attention. God loves the people who don't only give the lip service but do something practically. With such people the king is captivated; such are the people He likes to live with. This is why He said about David, that he is according to my heart (1-Samuel 13:14). For Daniel, He said, "greatly beloved man" (Daniel 10:11, 19) and for John the disciple it is written that he was the one whom Jesus loved (John 13:23, 21:7, 20).

7:6

How beautiful and how pleasant you are, love, for delights!

God enjoys when believers gather together and exalt His name. Jesus called His disciples His friends (John 15:15). Everyone rejoices in the company of his friends. We are friends of Jesus, and friends delight in the company of each other. So Jesus enjoys our company and we enjoy His companionship. For true friendship, the beauty of face doesn't matter. It is the beauty of hearts that joins two people. Jesus doesn't look at our physical face, shape, size, color, or nationality. He only looks at our hearts (Proverbs 11:20, 12:22). It is not the outward beauty of a person which makes them attractive to God but inward beauty. There is a very well-known verse in 2-Corinthians 9:7, *"…for God loves a cheerful giver"*. The emphasis in this verse is "cheerfulness", not "giving". Cheerfulness comes from our inner being which is related to the happiness of the heart. This happy feeling which comes from inside us attracts God and He delights in us. The emphasis is not on how much we give but how we give. He accepted the two small coins of the widow (Mark 12:41-44) but rejected the large offerings of King Balak (Numbers 22:40-41) because He looks at the motive with which we come into His presence. God's decision to accept or reject someone's sacrifice depends on the motive he is coming with.

He declared in Isaiah 1:13-14,

Bring no more vain offerings. Incense is an abomination to me. New moons, Sabbaths, and convocations: I can't stand evil assemblies. My soul hates your New Moons and your appointed feasts. They are a burden to me. I am weary of bearing them.

God Himself stipulated the offerings Israelites needed to bring on different feasts and on a daily basis. When the Israelites started bringing them with sin in their hearts and feeling that it was a burden for them, God didn't like it. Such offerings are a burden unto God. God doesn't respect such offerings and He doesn't delight in such gifts. His delight is in His own people; *"Yahweh takes pleasure in his people"* (Psalms 149:4). He created everything on this earth. All the animals on thousands of hills belong to God. He produces the yield of the earth (Psalms 104:27-30). If He had been hungry, He wouldn't ask you to bring anything. Anything and everything He needs, He can call and everything would come to Him (Psalms 50:7-15). The best gift He desires from us is the worship of our whole hearts (Hebrews 13:15). He delights in obedience more than any gift.

1 Samuel 15:22

Samuel said, "Has Yahweh as great delight in burnt offerings and sacrifices, as in obeying Yahweh's voice? Behold, to obey is better than sacrifice, and to listen than the fat of rams.

Lord God takes delight in His bride because they are the only people who obey Him. Obedience is the key to blessing. So He blesses His bride.

7:7

This, your stature, is like a palm tree, your breasts like its fruit.

A palm is a tall, strong, and deep-rooted tree that can stand in strong winds, bear wild weather, the extreme heat of the day and after bearing all the hardships it brings very sweet, tasty, and abundant fruit. All these are the attributes that we can see in a believer. Therefore, a palm tree represents a believer in the Bible. A believer is strong like a house on the rock (Luke 6:48). He can stand against the strong winds of temptation in the wilderness, when everyone else leaves him alone, he doesn't leave the grounds of his faith. Through his deep roots, he sucks the water of deeper revelations from the Word of God. He can bear the scorching heat of false accusations. No matter what his opponents say against him, he will be blessing them (Romans 12:14).

Psalm 92:12, *"The righteous shall flourish like the palm tree. He will grow like a cedar in Lebanon."*

In Isaiah 9:14, God compares the nobles of Israel with palm trees. In Solomon's temple, palm trees could be seen on the walls of the main hall (2- Chronicles 3:5, 1-Kings 6:35, 7:36). It was not only Solomon's temple where we could see the palm trees; we can see them in Ezekiel's temple as well (Ezekiel 40:16).

The bridegroom compared the bride's breasts with the clusters of fruit, or grapes (in some translations). Plenty of fruit, or grapes, in a harvest were considered as a blessing (Leviticus 26:3-5). A palm tree can be considered as one of the tallest fruit-bearing trees. Whereas other fruit-bearing plants like grapevines don't grow as tall as a palm tree. Grapevines represent believers in the Old and New Testament (Jeremiah 2:21, Isaiah 5:7, John 15:1-5).

If we combine the two similes of palm trees and clusters of fruit or grapes, we will see that believers are like a palm tree. It can be visible from a long distance. So it gives hope to the travelers in the desert that there is some food on the tree and they can rest in the shadow. Similarly, the church is a place where people will get spiritual food and rest from their burdens. A church is not only like a palm tree, it is like grapes as well. Grapes look tiny but they have great significance for men and God. Wine from grapes is used by men and it was used in burnt sacrifices as well. So the church is a place where people find hope, food, and rest in the form of palm trees and the church is also a place where people get their thirst quenched by the juice of grapes.

7:8

I said, "I will climb up into the palm tree. I will take hold of its fruit." Let your breasts be like clusters of the vine, the smell of your breath like apples.

To climb a tree, the climber has to start from the base, near the roots, and go up. The roots of a palm tree are visible quite high above the ground. When a climber climbs on a palm tree, he has to first climb the roots and then go upward towards the fruit. It means that when the climber goes up the tree, he has to go through all the parts of the tree. The palm tree represents the church. So by climbing the palm tree means that Jesus will visit each and every part of the church. The church is made up of different believers. Each believer is considered as a significant organ of the church body. The bridegroom climbing up the palm tree means that Jesus considers each and every believer as an important part of the body and He visits every one of us.

Believers are the fruit of the ministry. When Jesus says that *"He will take hold of its fruit"*, He means that He takes care of the new believers. After the resurrection, when Jesus met John, Jesus asked Him, *"Do you love me?"* When John answered "yes", Jesus gave him an assignment. Jesus asked him to take care of the lambs (John 21:15). Lambs are the young ones in any flock. These young ones are new believers. Jesus doesn't only visit the church to see the state of young believers but He also checks how fruitful our ministry is. The ministers, who work hard to raise the new believers to maturity, would be rewarded when Jesus will come back in His glory.

1-Thessalonians 2:19-20

For what is our hope, or joy, or crown of rejoicing? Isn't it even you, before our Lord Jesus at his coming? For you are our glory and our joy.

In the previous verse, we have already discussed the simile of clusters of grapes and breasts. In this verse, Jesus is comparing the breasts with the clusters of grapes that are attached to the vine. Jesus is the true vine and we are branches. True believers are the vine branches that are attached to the vine. They are getting the sap as their food and strength from the vine. Jesus wants each one of Jesus' children to be properly attached to Him. He doesn't want any other kind of attachment in our life. Breasts are the organs that release the milk which is used as food and strength of others. Jesus wants such believers in the church who don't only get their spiritual strength from Jesus but should become a channel of blessing for others as well. As Jesus said, *"He who believes in me, as the Scripture has said, from within him will flow rivers of living water."* (John 7:38).

The bridegroom's desire for His beloved is that her breath may have the smell of an apple. In Songs of Solomon 2:3, the bride likened the bridegroom to an apple tree. In Songs of Solomon 2:5, she said, *"refresh me with apples"*. The bride likes the apples so much that she compared her beloved with apples, and through apples, she gets refreshed. It seems that the bride and bridegroom have the same desire, because the bridegroom wants the breath of the bride to smell like an apple. Someone can only have the smell of an apple in his breath if he has just finished eating an apple. If the bridegroom always wants such a smell in her mouth then she always has to eat an apple. As Jesus is linked with an apple; so spiritually we can say that His bride (church) should have the smell of an apple (Jesus) in her breath. In other words when church people talk with someone they should have the smell of Jesus in their talk. When they go into the world, people may see a difference in their behavior, dealings, attitude, and conversation. They should be a living testimony of Jesus Christ.

7:9

Your mouth is like the best wine, that goes down smoothly for my beloved, gliding through the lips of those who are asleep.

This verse contains the words of both the bride and bridegroom. The first portion is the speech of the bridegroom and the second portion is the speech of the bride.

It is the overwhelming desire of the bridegroom that the mouth of the bride is like the best wine. It means the words which come out of the bride's mouth should have strong power in them, such that people may feel the effect of the best wine. The words of church leaders should have such a strong impact on the lives of hearers that people will want to ask for such teachings again and again like a highly effective wine. Jesus had this effect in His life. Wherever He went, large crowds drew to Him. In those days there was no social media, news channels, or internet. He did nothing for His media campaign or publicity; yet His fame spread everywhere. It was the Spirit of God that was drawing people to Him.

We often see, in the Word of God, that the Spirit of God attracts people to His servants. In Judges chapter 6, we read about Gideon. He was very much afraid of the enemy. When the Spirit of God came upon him, he got strength from God and favor from people. He blew the trumpet, gave the call for war and people from different parts of Israel gathered to him. On the Day of Pentecost Peter preached and three thousand people believed in Jesus. His words were effective like strong wine. In Acts Chapter 13 we see that Paul was preaching. His talk was so effective that people requested him to continue teaching the same topic next week. Next week almost the whole city gathered to listen to the words of God (Acts 13:44). It wasn't by Paul's own ability. It was the Holy Spirit who was gathering people and making his speech effective. Acts 13:49 tells us that the Word of God spread in that whole area. This is the kind of effectiveness Jesus wants in our speech.

The bridegroom wants our speech to be effective in and out of the church, like strong wine. The bride's desire is that this wine may go straight to the bridegroom. She wants a link between wine and bridegroom. As we have already discussed, this wine is the effectiveness in our speech which we get through the Holy Spirit. This wine or effectiveness is the result of the connection we have with the Holy Spirit. By going straight to the bridegroom means the target of our speech should be, Jesus. The words we utter should glorify Jesus and not our own efforts, success, or stories. Jesus is the miracle worker who made wine out of water in clay pots (John 2:1-12). We can relate servants in this story with the servants of God who sow the seed of the Word of God in our lives. That seed is like the water in clay jars which were at the wedding in Cana of Galilee. Our lives are the jars of clay. Jesus changes that water into wine. When we listen to the Word, it is just information but Jesus changes that information into revelation; which changes our destiny. Jesus is the one who converts the words which are coming from our mouth into life-saving speech. Its effect is like strong wine. This speech doesn't glorify anyone else; it glorifies only Jesus Christ. That's why the bride wishes that the wine may go straight to the bridegroom. It means the words we utter should be the words of worship.

The last part of this verse is, "gliding through the lips of those who are asleep". The wine or the Word of God doesn't affect lives forcefully. If someone doesn't accept it, it is like the wine which is flowing over the lips of sleepers. Best wine always costs a lot. People, who don't accept the Word of God, are like the people who are sleeping. They don't know that they are losing the chance to be filled up with a valuable but free wine. A time will come when they will leave this earth and go into the presence of God. They will be asked why they didn't accept the chance to be saved by the saving grace of our Lord Jesus Christ. At that time they will have no answer to cover up their shame.

7:10

I am my beloved's. His desire is toward me.

In this verse, the bride boldly declares that she belongs to her beloved. Our God is a God of purity. He doesn't want any diversions in our lives. Diversions in relation to our spouse or God leads to impurity. In the Old Testament, the punishment for deception in marital relations was death. Jesus is the bridegroom and we are His bride. If there is no purity in our relationship with Christ then we will have punishment in hell. He loves us like His children but His jealousy is like the jealousy of husband. He doesn't want His wife to wander around with other gods. He is a jealous God.

Deuteronomy 4:24, *"For Yahweh your God is a devouring fire, a jealous God."*

1-John 4:8, *"... God is love."*

There is a big debate in the modern world that asks "how can a loving father punish people in hell?" We know that all the animals and birds love their little ones. When we study small sparrows, if their chicks fall down from their nest, and someone puts them back, the sparrow will not accept that chick again. A lion feeds its children but kills other baby lions which are not his. If you touch the newborn of a rabbit, the rabbit mother will not accept that kid again. Your scent will be mixed with the scent of the baby and the mother will think that it is not her baby; so she will leave that baby alone. In the same way, when we come to God, He can sense that we have the smell of some other god and reject us, until we are washed with the blood of Christ. Love and jealousy are the two sides of the same coin. Love is not complete without jealousy. Love provides for us and jealousy takes away those provisions. Jealousy is not a bad emotion. If someone attacks or kidnaps your spouse then you go after him because of the love you have for her, but you fight for her because of the jealousy you have for her that no one may touch your spouse.

God has both jealousy and love. When we go to some other

god or we give preference to someone else, more than God then we become impure. Impurity in us prompts the anger and jealousy of God, but when we ask for forgiveness He accepts us because of the love He has for us. Some Bible scholars think that before the birth of Isaac, Abraham used to spend more time with God. When Isaac came into his life, Abraham started giving more time to Isaac as compared to God. If we give preference to someone other than God, then that thing or person becomes a god to us. God doesn't allow any Isaac in our life to take His place. That's why God commanded Abraham to offer Isaac as a sacrifice. He loves us as if we are the only ones in this universe, and He demands the same kind of dedication from us.

By saying that "I am my beloved's" (Song of Songs 7:10), she says that I am totally and fully dedicated to my God. She has the surety that her beloved also desires her. Jesus said that even if one sheep is left behind in the wilderness, He will go in search of that sheep. It means if I was the only sinner on this earth, still He would have come to give His life on the cross for me. His desire is for me, but His holiness would not accept anything less than holy. So to make me holy, He shed His blood, and to keep me walking in His holiness, He sent His Holy Spirit. He desires us so much that now He lives in believers through His Holy Spirit. The Holy Spirit sustains our spiritual life.

7:11

Come, my beloved! Let's go out into the field. Let's lodge in the villages.

The bride is requesting the bridegroom to go with her to the countryside and then spend the night in the villages. When the bride/ church requests something of God, it means they are spending time in prayer. From this verse, we can learn how and what a church should pray. In ministry, a follow-up is a necessary tool. When we select a place for outreach, we often pray to God before going for successful outreach. So we request God to be with us in this whole process. But what is our strategy after that outreach?

Throughout the ministry of Jesus, we can see that Jesus had been visiting Jerusalem and other cities again and again. Visiting a place again for ministry is known as follow-up. The bride is asking to visit the countryside and villages to follow up. She wants to visit those places with Christ. A ministry visit without Jesus is not a ministry at all; it would be nothing more than a business trip. She wants Jesus not only to visit those places but to spend the night over there. In Luke 24:13-32, Jesus was asked to spend the night with two people who were going on the road to Emmaus. While they were with Him, Jesus explained many scriptures to them. When Jesus met them they were very sad but when He finished the conversation, they were very happy. Their spiritual eyes were closed but when they understood the scriptures, their eyes were opened.

If Jesus is leading our outreaches and we request Him to stay in the villages, the lives of the people will be changed. The people who are stubborn will humble their hearts. Spiritual and physical eyes of people will be opened; sadness will leave our homes. Jesus went with Simon (spiritually) to the house of Cornelius and the joy of salvation came over them (Acts Chapter 10). Jesus was with Paul on the island of Malta; because of His presence, the whole island came to a saving knowledge of Jesus Christ (Acts Chapter 28). When Jesus was called by the sisters of Lazarus to their home, He raised their brother from death (John Chapter 11). If we will take Jesus with us on all our campaigns, we will have revival in the land.

7:12

Let's go early up to the vineyards. Let's see whether the vine has budded, its blossom is open, and the pomegranates are in flower. There I will give you my love.

This verse is the continuation of the previous verse where the bride asked the bridegroom to visit and stay in the countryside and villages. Now the bride is asking the bridegroom to visit the orchards; to see the condition of orchards. In Song of Songs 6:11, the bridegroom wanted to go to see the fruit trees of the orchards. As we saw in the previous verse, the request of the bride is a prayer to Jesus. She knows the will of the bridegroom. A key to successful prayer life is to pray according to the will of God.

1-John 5:14

This is the boldness which we have toward him, that if we ask anything according to his will, he listens to us.

The bride is asking something which is already settled in the will of Christ. He always wants to visit them. He wants to see if everything is going well with them. He doesn't want any disease or insect that may harm the trees of His orchard. He wants to eliminate anything which may harm the spiritual growth of His people. Fruitful trees represent righteous people or believers (John 15:5, Psalm 1:3). The diseases which can stop our fruit or growth are given in Galatians 5:19-21. The names of these diseases are sexual immorality, impurity, debauchery, idolatry, witchcraft, hatred, discord, jealousy, fits of rage, selfish ambition, dissensions, factions, envy, drunkenness, orgies, and the like.

Jesus is the best doctor. He knows all the spiritual and physical diseases. He also knows the medicine for them. He is so deep in His work that just by looking at someone He can diagnose the root cause of the disease. He looked at a wealthy man in Matthew 19:16-24. His wealth was a hindrance between him and God. Jesus prescribed the medicine that he should sell everything he has, give money to the poor, and follow Him. Jesus appeared to Solomon and told him that the disease of idolatry can take away his kingdom (1-Kings 11:1-13). He appeared to King Jeroboam but he didn't listen to God (1-Kings 14:1-11). In Genesis 4:4-7, Jesus examined Cain and told him that he was suffering from the disease of anger. Jesus is so passionate about His people that He always wants to be in contact with us to keep us safe from Satan. That's why He wanted to go and check the fruitful trees; that is the believers in this world. The bride knew the heart and mind of Christ so she asked Him to visit the orchard. He knows that the enemy always tries to distract us. The example of Job is before us.

The bride said that she will give Him her love when Jesus comes to the orchard. Jesus has given us a quick check to test if someone loves Him or not. This check can be called the obedience test. If someone loves Jesus, he will obey him.

John 14:15, *"If you love me, keep my commandments."*

When the bride says that I will give you my love, it means I will show you the level of obedience I have for your commands. The proof of that obedience can be seen in the form of flowers and fruits in the garden. Jesus commanded in Matthew 28:19-20 to make disciples in all the nations. If we love Him then we will obey His command to save people from the kingdom of darkness. The souls saved would be the fruit we bear and it will be the proof of our love for Him. Our duty is not finished when someone accepts Christ. The next phase of the duty is that we need to take care of those people until they mature in Christ. This maturity is judged by the fruit they will bear. That's why the bride requests the bridegroom to have a look at the flowers and fruit in the orchard; the fruit which new believers are bringing, giving proof of their maturity. When the church prepares new people to bring fruit into God's kingdom; it is showing its respect and loves it has for Christ.

7:13

The mandrakes produce fragrance. At our doors are all kinds of precious fruits, new and old, which I have stored up for you, my beloved.

Other than Song of Songs, the only place we see the word "mandrakes" is in Genesis 30:14; where Leah and Rachel fought over the mandrakes. Mandrake is used to treat different illnesses. It also helps in increasing interest in sexual activity. In Song of Songs 7:11-12, the bride invited the bridegroom to the orchard. When the bridegroom came she said that I have the best fruits gathered for you. These are dried and fresh fruits. Dried fruits can last for a longer period of time whereas fresh fruits like watermelon and apples can't last for that long.

By combining all the information given in this verse, we understand that the bride is trying her best to honor the bridegroom. By mentioning mandrakes, she is saying that she is ready to offer herself to bring a new generation into this world. Church people should always keep themselves available for the sake of evangelism. Through evangelism, we can keep on bringing the new generation of believers into this world. No matter in what state and where we are, we need to evangelize the people. Paul was in prison when he wrote many letters to the churches at that time. He is still evangelizing through those epistles because they are part of the New Testament, and in this way, they have been blessing the world for hundreds of years. He was in chains but the Word of God wasn't in chains. He had been evangelizing the soldiers who were on guard duty (Philippians 1:12-14). When he was presented to the king and officials, without fearing for his life, he preached the gospel over them.

Acts 26:28-29

Agrippa said to Paul, "With a little persuasion are you trying to make me a Christian?" Paul said, "I pray to God, that whether with little or with much, not only you, but also all that hear me today, might become such as I am, except for these bonds."

The word "fruit" in the Bible is not only used for physical food or fruit. Symbolically, it is also used for different acts and their results (Jeremiah 32:19, Proverbs 18:20, Matthew 3:8). In some places, this word is also used to represent the fruit of the body, which is physical children (Deuteronomy 28:53, Lamentations 2:20). When Jesus was talking about false prophets, He said, *"Therefore by their fruits you will know them."* (Matthew 7:20). So when the bride says that she has gathered new and old delicacies or dried and fresh fruits, it means to look at my previous and present work. I had been faithful to you and I will remain faithful to you till the end. I have been bringing people to your kingdom and I will keep on doing my work. You can't rescue someone from the kingdom of darkness until you rout that kingdom from his life (Matthew 12:29). Through evangelism and spiritual warfare, we attack the kingdom of darkness and bring people to the kingdom of light. By offering the fruit, the bride is saying that I have been serving you in the past. My love for you is pure. Its intensity is increasing with the passage of time. Your passion to save the lost souls is now my passion. Your desires are my desires and it is an honor for me to keep on serving you throughout my life.

8

8:1

Oh that you were like my brother, who nursed from the breasts of my mother! If I found you outside, I would kiss you; yes, and no one would despise me.

After reading this verse, some people are confused as to why the bride is saying that it would be better if you would be my brother. In fact, she does not desire that the bridegroom should be her brother, but she desires the liberty she would have with Him, outside the home. If she were to kiss her brother openly in the street, no one would have despised her. Maybe some of the people would admire her for loving her brother so much.

A mother loves and cares for her newborn baby so much that she spends most of her time with the baby. Similarly, a newlywed couple like to spend most of their time with each other. They spend almost all the time with each other. Sometimes other people make fun of them because they always want to stay together, holding hands, like they are in some other world. In some cultures, this kind of expression of love is not acceptable. They want that outside the home, a man should always show his supremacy over the woman and they can come close to each other only behind closed doors. In public, they are not allowed even to hold each other's hands. However, if a mother is going about with her son, she can kiss him or hold his hand in public. A sister can also show her affection by kissing her brother in public.

By saying, "Oh that you were like my brother", she is saying that I wish to express my love to you everywhere in all circumstances. The same emotion was expressed by Paul when he said, "*Who shall separate us from the love of Christ? Could oppression, or anguish, or persecution, or famine, or nakedness, or peril, or sword?*" (Romans 8:35). The same kind of emotions was expressed by David in Psalms. Psalm 42:2, "*My soul thirsts for God, for the living God. When shall I come and appear before God?*" Psalm 27:4, "*One thing I have asked of Yahweh, that I will seek after: that I may dwell in Yahweh's house all the days of my life, to see Yahweh's beauty, and to inquire in his temple.*"

The woman, who poured out the expensive perfume on Jesus' feet, expressed her love despite the opposition she faced from people. Although Jesus was living in a conservative culture, even then the ladies didn't leave Him when He was being led off to be crucified because they loved Him, and the love they had for Him was stronger than the disapproval of the culture. In the time of Jesus, it looked awkward if a man talked to an unfamiliar lady. Jesus didn't worry about what the people would say about Him. He talked with an unfamiliar lady who didn't have a good reputation among the people for living with a man not her husband (John 4:5-27). It is not only the bride who doesn't want to consider any kind of disapproval of her relationship with the bridegroom. Jesus also doesn't want any hindrance between Himself and His bride; this is why He didn't hesitate to have fellowship with sinners and tax collectors (Matthew 9:9-12, 11:19).

8:2

I would lead you, bringing you into the house of my mother, who would instruct me. I would have you drink spiced wine, of the juice of my pomegranate.

The bride wishes that she could bring the bridegroom to her mother's house. She would listen to the instructions of her mother and she would serve the best drink, the wine of pomegranate. When we look at these words in the context of the present-day environment, it is a lesson for young couples that they shouldn't think only about themselves. They should involve the parents in their happy moments. Parents may have sacrificed many things for their children, so the children should also think about their parents when they make decisions about their lives. The bride wishes to bring her bridegroom into her home to meet the family members there. A successful married life is not only a happy relationship between husband and wife. A good relationship with each other's families would be a bonus for them and the circle of their happiness would be widened.

If we talk spiritually then the church is the mother of believers because a church cares for young believers and they are born out of the efforts of the church. The bride wanted the bridegroom to come to her home. Every believer is a part of the church and the church as a whole is his spiritual mother. It should be the desire of every believer that Jesus may come and visit his home church. When Jesus was on this earth there were many synagogues (Jewish worship places) in Israel, but Jesus wasn't happy with most of them. At one point Jesus called their religious leaders white washed graves (Matthew 23:27). The graves looked beautiful from the outside but are filled with filth from inside. Jesus didn't like those worship places and leaders because their worship services were lacking the presence of God. Without the presence of God our worship places are no more than secular meeting places. It is the presence of God which converts a building into a worship place. Without His presence, a church is no better than the worship place of any other religion. A manger with Jesus is better than Herod's palace without Jesus. Moses left Pharaoh's palace and went to the Israelites' camp in poverty because they were rich in God's presence.

When the bride wishes that the bridegroom should visit her house, it shows the desire of a believer that God's presence may visit the church he is attending. It is not only the duty of the pastor to pray for the tangible presence of Jesus in the church. It is the duty of every believer that we may request Jesus to visit us every time we meet. There was a lady who had been suffering from a disease for eighteen years (Luke 13:10-17). She had been crippled by a spirit for eighteen years. For eighteen years she was attending the meetings in the synagogue but one day Jesus came there, this was the day of her release. Do we wish that amazing works may happen in our churches? Then invite Jesus as the bride invited Him to visit her mother's house, which is her church.

Every word which is written in the Bible is important. After expressing the wish that the bridegroom may come to visit her house, she wishes that her mother may teach her in the presence of the bridegroom. It is very desirable because any teaching without the presence of Jesus is not successful. It could be good knowledge but not revelation. Knowledge may change someone's life but revelation changes their destination. Jesus had twelve disciples and Jesus asked them *"Who do men say that I, the Son of Man, am?"* Different disciples gave him different answers. It was only Peter, who had the revelation of Jesus and answered, *"You are the Christ, the Son of the living God."* Because of this revelation, Jesus said, *"On this rock I will build my assembly, and the gates of Hades will not prevail against it"*.

Peter wasn't the rock; it was the revelation that Peter received. The church is built on the revelation that Jesus is the Son of God. We get revelation in the presence of Jesus. This is why the bride desired that Jesus should come to her mother's house. The mother's house is the church where we go. With Jesus in the church and church leaders preaching in the church, people will have the strong base of the Word of God and His church will keep on building upon the basis of these revelations.

The bride wanted to offer the bridegroom spiced wine made from the juice of her pomegranates. Wine is not prepared overnight. It takes quite some time to make good wine because the juice which is extracted from pomegranates needs some time to be processed. In previous chapters, we discussed that pomegranates represent the Word of God. In this verse we see that first, the bride wanted the bridegroom to come to her house then she wanted to be taught by her mother. Those teachings are the revelations of the Word of God. Now she wants to offer something which is the extract of the fruit. When we listen to the Word, it goes into our soul and becomes a revelation for our spirit. This process takes some time like the process of winemaking; once it is processed, we can present it to Jesus. Moses got the Word from God.

Exodus 3:7-8

"Yahweh said, "I have surely seen the affliction of my people who are in Egypt, and have heard their cry because of their taskmasters, for I know their sorrows. I have come down to deliver them out of the hand of the Egyptians, and to bring them up out of that land to a good and large land, to a land flowing with milk and honey; to the place of the Canaanite, the Hittite, the Amorite, the Perizzite, the Hivite, and the Jebusite."

According to the above two verses, God promised that He will deliver His people and take His people to the Promised Land. When the Israelites disobeyed God, Moses took hold of this Word and interceded for the Israelites (Exodus 32:14). This was the wine Moses presented to the bridegroom. Moses received the Word, meditated on it and when it was processed under the Spirit of God, it became revelation. The same word in the form of revelation acted like the spiced wine. This received word became the perceived word and was presented to God. In Acts 1:15-26, Peter encouraged the believers to choose a disciple to fill the place left vacant by Judas Iscariot. Peter used the scriptures given in Psalm 69:25 and Psalm 109:8-15. He received the revelation of these scriptures. The written Word became a revelation like juice converts into wine. This wine or revelation was brought before men and God, and both accepted it. God accepted it in the form of prayer because they prayed based on that word and people accepted it as the inspired word of God.

8:3

His left hand would be under my head. His right hand would embrace me.

Here we see the closeness the bride and bridegroom have. When two people embrace each other, it means no one else is between them. Parents always wish their children well, but Genesis 2:24 says, "*Therefore a man will leave his father and his mother, and will join with his wife, and they will be one flesh.*" Such closeness in the Bible is symbolized with prayer.1-Corinthians 6:16-17, "*Or don't you know that he who is joined to a prostitute is one body? For, "The two", he says, "will become one flesh." But he who is joined to the Lord is one spirit.*"

In prayer we unite with the Lord; this unity is known as oneness in spirit. Moses experienced this closeness when he stayed on the mountain for forty days without water and food. A man can't live without food and water for forty days. We can live without food for forty days but not without water. God doesn't need food and water to live. Moses didn't need food while he was spending time with God (Exodus 34:28). A supernatural strength was provided to Moses; and real supernatural strength only resides with God. When Moses received that strength (in a limited way) to live without food, that means God's strength was flowing in him. This is how we become one with God.

Hannah prayed so intensely that she became unaware of her

surroundings. It was just God, and her passion for God. She poured out her heart for God (1-Samuel 1:12-17). She didn't care if someone was taking notice of her not. First, she came to God, and later God came to the whole nation through her. She gave birth to Samuel and through Samuel, God visited the whole nation. When Samuel was a child, the Israelites were so far from God that He stopped communicating with them (1-Samuel 3:1). When Samuel grew up, he had a passion for his nation. After this we see in 1-Samuel 19:20, "group of prophets". Prophets are the people who speak on behalf of God. God used to communicate with people through prophets. In 1-Samuel 19:20, this group of prophets was prophesying. How did this change come about in Israel? First, we read in 1-Samuel 3:1, "*Yahweh's word was rare in those days*". But, in 1-Samuel 19:20, prophets were openly prophesying. We don't see any other person at that time except Samuel who was so near to God. So this revival was the result of Samuel's prayers for his nation. This whole thing started with one lady who was sincere with God and became one with Him through her prayers.

The extreme example of being one with God is the life of Jesus. All His actions were in accordance with God's will; He said, *"Most certainly, I tell you, the Son can do nothing of himself, but what he sees the Father doing. For whatever things he does, these the Son also does likewise*" (John 5:19). Jesus never imagined a single second living without the fellowship of His father. The only time the father made Himself separate from Jesus was when He was bearing the sins of the whole world. God can't live with sin, so He left His only son. This separation was hard for Jesus to bear. He cried with a loud voice and died. He didn't want to live even a single second on this earth without the fellowship of His father. We are the bride of Christ. We shouldn't live a life without Him. Through prayer, He embraces us and we become one with Him in spirit.

8:4

I adjure you, daughters of Jerusalem, that you not stir up, nor awaken love, until it so desires.

The bridegroom is sleeping but the bridegroom is Jesus. He had been sleeping only in his earthly life because he was living as a human. When He rose up from the dead, he rose as God. *For to this end Christ died, rose, and lived again, that he might be Lord of both the dead and the living* (Romans 14:9). Being God, He never sleeps. "*He will not allow your foot to be moved. He who keeps you will not slumber. Behold, he who keeps Israel will neither slumber nor sleep*" (Psalm 121:3-4).

In His earthly life, He never scolded anyone for disturbing Him. He had been working hard in His earthly life. When we study His life deeply, we see that several times He had been preaching and serving the people for long hours, and sometimes they didn't have time to rest or eat.

Mark 6:31

"He said to them, "You come apart into a deserted place, and rest awhile." For there were many coming and going, and they had no leisure so much as to eat"

Because so many people had been coming to Jesus, He and the disciples hardly got time to rest, yet even then He always wanted to bless humanity. If anybody tried to hinder people from coming to Him, He scolded that person because we are the bride of Christ and He always kept Himself available for His bride. When people brought their children to Jesus and disciples tried to stop them, Jesus scolded His disciples. At that time He said the famous verse, "*Allow the little children to come to me, and don't hinder them, for God's Kingdom belongs to such as these*" (Luke 18:16).

Jesus always welcomed people when they come to Him but there is an incident where Jesus scolded those who came to Him. They were none other than His disciples. Jesus was sleeping in the boat and there was a storm in the sea. Disciples became worried so they woke up Jesus.

Matthew 8:23-26

"When he got into a boat, his disciples followed him. Behold, a violent storm came up on the sea, so much that the boat was covered with the waves; but he was asleep. The disciples came to him and woke him up, saying, "Save us, Lord! We are dying!" He said to them, "Why are you fearful, O you of little faith?" Then he got up, rebuked the wind and the sea, and there was a great calm."

Do you think that Jesus rebuked His disciples for disturbing Him while He was sleeping? It was not the disturbance by disciples that angered Jesus; it was the lack of faith in their lives which made Jesus angry. It is clear that in His earthly life Jesus was never bothered by people coming to Him but He disliked the people coming without faith. Therefore when the bride charges the daughters of Jerusalem, not to awaken her love; she doesn't mean that Jesus is sleeping in reality and that she is forbidding the ladies from awaking Him.

Daughters of Jerusalem are the believers. When Jesus was crucified, some ladies were there who came with Jesus and they were the supporters of Jesus' ministry. Jesus called them daughters of Jerusalem.

Luke 23:27-28

A great multitude of the people followed him, including women who also mourned and lamented him. But Jesus, turning to them, said, "Daughters of Jerusalem, don't weep for me, but weep for yourselves and for your children.

When the bride requests the daughters of Jerusalem not to disturb the bridegroom; it means she is asking the believers to stand in faith because faithlessness in the church disturbs Him a lot. The people outside the church are faithless people; there is no doubt about that, but people inside the church without faith, hurt Jesus. A dishonest friend hurts more than an enemy. Similarly, people in the church without faith hurt Him more than the people outside the church. Calling ourselves faithful and doing the acts of faithlessness, grieves Jesus. So the bride is requesting the people in the church that do not grieve Jesus. By the words "*until it so desires*", means let Jesus do the work as He wishes; according to His timing. For God, some people say that God is never late and He is never early. His timing is fixed and perfect but, being humans, sometimes we want everything to be done briskly. God had time to take the Israelites out of Egypt (Genesis 15:13). He decreed seventy years for the Israelites' slavery in Babylon (Jeremiah 25:11-12, Daniel 9:2). He had a fixed timing in His plan for Jesus to be born, crucified, and resurrected (Romans 5:6, Galatians 4:4). If we are going through some kind of test, trial or tribulation then have faith God will take you out and set you free at His best time.

8:5

Who is this who comes up from the wilderness, leaning on her beloved? Under the apple tree I awakened you. There your mother conceived you. There she was in labor and bore you.

This verse has two portions. In the first portion, friends looked at the bride and bridegroom. The bride was walking with the bridegroom and she is leaning on the bridegroom. In the second portion, the bridegroom talks with the bride and said that He wakes her up under the apple tree. Christ is the head of the church (Ephesians 5:23, 1:22). The church has to look to Christ for all its needs, in this way church is leaning on Christ. We are leaning on Christ because we are totally dependent on Christ. When we depend on Christ then He is responsible for everything. Step by step, He takes us to our destination. God didn't take David directly from shepherd to king. David had to move one step at a time. He had to trust God every time, whether living in the palace enjoying his friendship with Jonathan or whether running from King Saul, or fighting with giants. When we completely trust in God it means we are leaning on God.

The life of Prophet Elijah is a good example of dependence on God. On God's order, he stopped the rain and on His order, he prayed for the rain to come (1-Kings 17:1). God told him to stay in the wilderness where God fed him through crows (1-Kings 17:6). Crows don't share their food with anyone. It was a great miracle that crows brought food for a long time, even when there was a shortage of food in the land. We know that the king Ahab tried to find him everywhere but he was not able to find Elijah (1-Kings 18:10). God kept his life safe by maintaining the secrecy about his whereabouts. No one would ever think to find Elijah by following the crows. At God's time, God commanded him to go and live with a widow and her son (1-Kings 17:8-9). After killing Baal's prophets, the queen wanted to kill him (1-Kings 19:1-3). At God's command, he anointed Elisha in his place to be a prophet. According to God's will, he was taken into heaven. In this way throughout his life, he was leaning on God.

The bride was leaning on the bridegroom and coming from the wilderness. There could be different wildernesses in our lives; where we feel ourselves alone and desire to die. But, these are the feelings when we are away from God. If we shift our focus from wilderness to Jesus, we will live a contented life. For forty years His bride Israel had been walking through the wilderness. At different occasions, in different problems when they put their focus on wilderness, they grumbled against God but when they changed their focus from wilderness to God, their problems were solved and they praised God. They had to lean on God for their security, food, water, shelter, and everything they needed. Whenever they left God and depended on their own intellect and wisdom, they fell down. They fell in idolatry and sometimes at the hands of the enemy. Depend on God: He has the power to change the wilderness into green pasture (Isaiah 32:15-16).

Isaiah 29:17-20

"Isn't it yet a very little while, and Lebanon will be turned into a fruitful field, and the fruitful field will be regarded as a forest? In that day, the deaf will hear the words of the book, and the eyes of the blind will see out of obscurity and out of darkness. The humble also will increase their joy in Yahweh, and the poor among men will rejoice in the Holy One of Israel. For the ruthless is brought to nothing, and the scoffer ceases, and all those who are alert to do evil are cut off."

The bridegroom roused the bride under the apple tree. We have seen that several times in Song of Songs, Jesus is symbolized as an apple tree and the church is the mother of believers. When Jesus says that He roused us under the apple tree, it means we were in His knowledge when we were born spiritually in the church. He knows the time and place of every believer when he accepted Christ and was born spiritually.

Psalm 87:5-6

"Yes, of Zion it will be said, "This one and that one was born in her;" the Most High himself will establish her. Yahweh will count, when he writes up the peoples, "This one was born there."

Zion represents the church in the Bible. God says that He keeps the record of people who were born in Zion. He knows the people who have the experience of new birth in their lives. He writes the name of every believer in the book of life at the time of repentance (Revelation 3:5, 21:27). Every believer, whose name is written in the Book of the Lamb, is the result of someone's prayer. Different people had been praying for our salvation. Some people had been fasting for us and praying for us when we were having a good night's sleep in our cosy beds. They had been awake and weeping for us. These are the labor pains that intercessors had to bear for spiritual birth to take place. The apostle talks about these pains in Galatians 4:19, "*My little children, of whom I am again in travail until Christ is formed in you*". Believers have to suffer through these pains that other believers may be born in the kingdom of God.

Jesus roused us under the apple tree. We know in Song of Songs Jesus is represented as an apple tree so in this verse the apple tree is the presence of God and the church is our spiritual mother. Once we are born again in the kingdom of God then we should not be sleeping spiritually. There is not much difference between a sleeping believer and a non-believer. In the parable of ten virgins, five of them were sleeping when the bridegroom came. The bridegroom left them out of the banquet hall and closed the door. He wants His bride to be awake and alert all the time, like a soldier on the battlefield. Therefore He awakens His bride; sometimes through sermons in church and sometimes through trials and tribulations.

8:6

Set me as a seal on your heart, as a seal on your arm; for love is strong as death. Jealousy is as cruel as Sheol. Its flashes are flashes of fire, a very flame of Yahweh.

There is a debate among Bible scholars about this verse. Some scholars believe that the words of this verse are the words of the bride and some think that these are the words of the bridegroom. I personally believe that these are the words of the bridegroom. Throughout history, we see that God remains faithful to His people, but His people often go astray from Him. If we keep this fact in mind then the bride doesn't need to utter the words, "*Set me as a seal on your heart*". These words are meaningful if Christ says these words because He knows that we often fall in sin (Romans 3:23,

Isaiah 53:6, Psalm 119:176). So we will study this verse keeping in mind that these words are spoken by the bridegroom.

The seal shows the ownership or authority over some object or order passed by an officer. Jesus advised the bride to keep Him as a seal on her heart. Sealed objects are only allowed by the owner to be opened; this is why Jesus' tomb was sealed by the Roman government that no one could open it. Jesus is asking her to keep her heart pure for Jesus. A seal on the arm was used as an ornament (Exodus 35:22, Numbers 31:50); but it was also used to reveal someone's identity (Genesis 38:18-25). When the bride wears the seal on her arm with the name of Jesus on it then everyone who looks at her will recognize that she belongs to Jesus. The seal on an arm is visible and outward, whereas seal on the heart is invisible and inward. Jesus doesn't want that our Christianity may have only outward effect; He wants the same kind of effect inward. The Pharisees and teachers of the law appeared Godly on the outside, but from inside they were filled with unrighteousness. So Jesus called them "whitewashed tombs". According to the Law of Moses, tombs, graves, and dead people were considered unholy (Numbers 19:16). So Jesus was telling them that if your inward appearance is different from your outward appearance, then you are a hypocrite and unholy person. Therefore church people must have holiness inwardly as well as outwardly.

The love of Christ is strong. It is so strong that He bore the cross. He gave His life because He loved us. To save us, He left His glory and came to this earth to be crucified for our sake. If His love is strong, His Jealousy is as strong as His love. Because, if God is love; He is a Jealous God as well (Exodus 34:14). When people go to other gods it invokes God's jealousy (Joshua 24:19). God counts it as spiritual adultery. Idolatry in the Bible is spiritual adultery. God hates idolatry. This was the prime reason for which God sent His people into exile (Psalm 78:55-62).

Love and jealousy are like two sides of a two-edged sword. If God punishes because of His jealousy, He saves because of His love. We see this pattern in God's dealings throughout history.

In almost all the history books in the Bible, we see that often the Israelites chose foreign gods. God became angry because of their acts and punished them by allowing the foreign troops to occupy their land, houses and vineyards, and they remained in slavery. But whenever they repented, God saved them because of His unfailing love (2-Kings 19:16-19).

8:7

Many waters can't quench love, neither can floods drown it. If a man would give all the wealth of his house for love, he would be utterly scorned.

Water has immense power. Water can save lives when we use it properly but it can destroy villages and even cities. If you go and visit the area where a flood has passed, you will see the destruction there. Flood wipes away the strong and big buildings on its way. After a flood, it will be difficult to say that once some buildings were standing at this place.

The bible says that love has more power than floods; nothing can sweep it away. Normally humans have a problem. Their love seems very strong but with the passage of time, it loses its grip. We see the same situation in the case of Amnon and Tamar in 2-Samuel 13:1-21. Amnon loved Tamar so much that he was ready to do anything for her. He was obsessed to such a degree that he fell ill. He used some inappropriate ways to get her but after having her for some time, he started hating her. His hate was even greater than his love. After ruining her life, he forced her out of his house. This is the problem in human behaviour, that love doesn't remain constant. Its level goes up and down. In Revelation 2:4, Jesus was addressing the church of Ephesus. He said, "*But I have this against you, that you left your first love.*" Jesus wants the same strong love from each one of us we had in the beginning when we were saved. Maybe at that time we were spending more time with God but not now. His love never decreases and He wants the same from us.

Sin has the same power in our lives as heavy floods. It can wipe away many blessings we have. But there is another reality, no matter how strong the flood of sin is, it can never sweep out the love God has for us. Romans 5:20 says, "*but where sin abounded, grace abounded more exceedingly*". In spite of our sins, he never breaks His covenants.

Jeremiah 31:37

"Yahweh says: "If heaven above can be measured, and the foundations of the earth searched out beneath, then I will also cast off all the offspring of Israel for all that they have done," says Yahweh."

God doesn't only teach us the laws which govern our spiritual lives; He also teaches us the rules to apply in our earthly lives. We need to be careful in our love relationships. Often the things are not as simple or good as they look. There are hundreds of examples where people gave everything they earned to people they love but the other person breaks the trust. Then the person who is deceived becomes a joke for everyone. In the book of Judges we see that Samson revealed the most precious secret of his life to Delilah in the name of love. His beloved deceived him and he became a person of ridicule in the eyes of all the people. We need to be careful while giving our possessions in the name of love. Maybe the other person is not sincere with you and wants to use you for his selfish gain. So we need to move with prayer and fasting while selecting our life partner. Personally, I will advise you to choose a Godly person under the guidance of the Holy Spirit. Don't be unevenly yoked.

8:8

We have a little sister. She has no breasts. What shall we do for our sister in the day when she is to be spoken for?

These are the words of friends or brothers of the bride. In Biblical times most of the marriages were arranged marriages. Arranged marriages have their own benefits. These days most people prefer love marriages. When we look at the records, we see that in the era of arranged marriages, the ratio of divorce was much less as compared to the people who have love marriages. In this verse, we see the scenario of arranged marriage. The good thing about arranged marriage is that different people think about the good future of a single person. Now, when we have a project of three months or six months, we involve different experienced people to help us in completing it. But, when we have to decide on our whole life, we like to handle it single-handedly.

One of the things we learn from this verse is that we should be careful about our children's marital life right from their childhood. We should train them slowly so that they may have a successful married life in the future. We send them to good schools and colleges so that they may have a successful professional life. But, married life is more important than professional life. Professional life and married life are both important to us, but professional life ends in a few years whereas a marriage lasts for our whole life.

Brothers are making plans to secure the future of their sister. A superb plan is given in Proverbs 22:6, *"Train up a child in the way he should go, and when he is old he will not depart from it."* Samuel is a good example of raising children in Godly ways. He kept on walking in God's principles till the end of his days. The brothers of the bride expressed their concern that when someone will ask about their sister to be married to his relative, what are the things they should keep in mind? If they are talking about their sister, that doesn't mean we shouldn't think about the marriage of our boys or that we need to devote effort for the girls only. Both girls and boys are equally important. We see such a condition in Genesis chapter 24. The whole chapter teaches us how we should make decisions in such a scenario. Abraham wanted to marry his son. He trusted his servant to handle the matter. He instructed him to go to Abraham's own people and bring a girl from there for his son to be his wife. Two things we can learn from here. First, we should prefer our own people, people who know our God. Abraham strictly ordered his servant that he shouldn't take a wife for his son from the Canaanites and he shouldn't take his son to Mesopotamia; because at both places, people were worshiping other gods. To go there meant accepting their gods but bringing someone from there means introducing someone to the real God. So while choosing a life partner the basic quality we should look for in someone is "salvation"; 1-Corinthians chapter 7 discusses these issues in detail.

Or God cares for us in each and every matter. We should involve Him in choosing the right partner. Joseph wanted to leave Mary but God told Joseph to marry Mary because He knows who the right partner for us is. We can be mistaken in choosing or rejecting someone. So ask Him to help you through His angels. Abraham prayed to God and He sent His angel to find a girl for Abraham's son Isaac. If He can send His angel for Isaac to select a wife, He can do it for you as well, because God does not show favoritism (Galatians 2:6).

8:9

If she is a wall, we will build on her a turret of silver. If she is a door, we will enclose her with boards of cedar.

In Biblical times and in some parts of the world even now, brothers or male residents of a house were considered as the protectors of the ladies and households in a house. In above verse we see that brothers are taking their responsibility. They are saying that they will be observing their sister closely; to know her behaviour, intentions, likeness, and character. Some people may think the brothers are overreacting but in reality, if you really love someone, you will observe all these character traits. People can't be changed by force, but love can turn them around. Christians are not against the personal liberty of choice. In fact, the level of liberty Christianity offers is not available in any other religion. There are religions in the world, if you leave them and accept some other religion, they will come after you to kill you. In Christianity, if you leave and go to some other religion, they will not kill you. They will counsel you, pray for you and wait for your eyes to be open to come back to Jesus but they will never force or kill you. When we talk about having a closer look at our children it doesn't mean we are restricting their liberty. It simply means we want to protect them until they become able to move in real liberty.

There are only two ways in life. One way goes towards Jesus who leads to heaven and others go away from Jesus, where Satan is waiting for the people to send them to hell. There is no place in between these two. Either you are on God's side or on Satan's side. While discussing their sister, the brothers knew that there are only two ways. She will follow only one of them. If she will follow the right path, she will be like a wall, but if her lifestyle ignores wisdom, then she will be like a door.

The wall around a city or a house ensures its protection. Comparing their sister with a wall proves that in the Bible, women are highly esteemed. Watchtowers are not made on the walls of houses. They are made on the walls of forts, palaces, or city walls. This shows a Godly lady is a protection for her people. She protects them from foreign intruders. When she bows before God and intercede for her family, she becomes a blessing for them. The towers mentioned in this verse are of silver and made by her brothers. Towers play a key role in the defence of a city. They are not used only to monitor the movement of the enemy; they are also used to inform the city people about attacking forces. They were also used to launch an arrow attack on the enemy. A praying daughter is the blessing in a house. She can get guidance from God and inform her people about the devil's plans. She can shoot arrows through her prayers on any demonic attack against her family because the weapons we fight with are not the weapons of the world. On the contrary, they have divine power to demolish strongholds (2-Corinthians 10:4). The towers are not made of bricks but of silver by the brothers. In the Bible, silver represents salvation. But, these towers are made by her brothers. It means her brothers will stand by their sister and teach her the way of salvation. They will teach her in a way that she becomes a blessing for others to lead them to salvation.

The other thing mentioned by the brothers is that their sister could behave like a door. A door is a way through which anyone can come in or go out. It means if their sister will not behave responsibly then they will close that way with the panels of cedar. Some people like the cedar roof and floor because its smell keeps snakes away. But enclosing her with cedar panels doesn't mean that brothers will put her in some kind of prison. We can't send someone to prison to keep them away from sin. The prophet Jeremiah gave its solution in Lamentations 2:19.

Arise, cry out in the night, at the beginning of the watches! Pour out your heart like water before the face of the Lord. Lift up your hands toward him for the life of your young children, who faint for hunger at the head of every street.

Jeremiah pleaded with his people to intercede for their children so that they may not die or go into slavery. If we will not intercede for our brothers, sisters, children, and nation, they can die a spiritual death or they can go in spiritual slavery. By using cedar panels mean we will use our prayers to block the way of Satan who wants to take our children away from God.

8:10

I am a wall, and my breasts like towers, then I was in his eyes like one who found peace.

In the last verse, we talked about the difference between a door and a wall. A wall is used for the separation and protection of the people. The bride said that she is a wall. She considers herself a responsible woman; a woman who separates her family from the rest of the world to protect them for their good. Proverbs 31:10-31, describes the characteristics of such a woman. She cares for her children and husband. Her husband believes in her abilities. She doesn't only take interest in everyday household work, but beyond that she does the business and manages the workers. Because of her efforts, her husband and children praise her. She is a woman who protects her family like a wall. In 1-Samuel 25, we see a woman whose name was Abigail. She was a wise woman when David became angry with her husband, Nabal. He wanted to kill all the male members of Nabal's household. Abigail hurried up and through her wisdom, she convinced David not to kill anyone. In this scenario, she acted like a wall around her family.

The breasts of the bride are like towers. This doesn't only show that she is ready to be married, it has some other meanings as well. Breasts are used to feed the little ones and towers are used to protect some areas. Apostle Peter compares milk with the Word of God (1-Peter 2:2). By combining these facts we know that the bride is saying that she will feed the spiritual children, or the people who accept Christ as their saviour, with spiritual food which helps them to move towards spiritual maturity. Her breasts are like towers means, through her teachings; believers would be able to recognise the moves of the devil from an early age. We shouldn't wait for children to reach the age of maturity to teach them about our spiritual enemy, Satan. Satan will not wait to destroy or distract them until they become mature. Therefore right from their childhood, we need to teach them the difference between good and evil. Sunday schools and bedtime stories are a good way to bring up our children in a Godly way. While walking on the road we hold hands of our child to keep them safe from the traffic nearby. Unconsciously we are teaching them the principles of walking on the road. For spiritual growth, we should start feeding them right from their early childhood.

We plan to wait to teach spiritual truths to children at a certain age. But God's plans are very different. In Genesis 12:1-3, God talked about Abraham's decedents; they were not born yet. God had plans for us hundreds of years before we were born. We are not in this world by some accident, we were in God's plan and He selected the tasks to be done by us before we were conceived in our mother's womb. The psalmist gives a very good description of this fact.

Psalm 139:14-17

"I will give thanks to you, for I am fearfully and wonderfully made. Your works are wonderful. My soul knows that very well. My frame wasn't hidden from you, when I was made in secret, woven together in the depths of the earth. Your eyes saw my body. In your book they were all written, the days that were ordained for me, when as yet there were none of them. How precious to me are your thoughts, God! How vast is their sum!"

Before anybody was able to see us, God was looking at us in our mother's womb. He was happy with us. He considered us a useful tool for His kingdom. He had plans for us. When we are physically born on this earth, He doesn't want to wait long for us to come into His presence. That is why according to Moses' Law on the eighth day of his birth; they have to circumcise the male child and give him a name (Luke 1:59, 2:21). Circumcision means that this child is a member of the covenant people (Israel). By giving a name to a child, we give an identity to that child. God wanted our children to be known as the part of the covenant community, His people, with a specific identity. We were in His eyes even before our birth, so by giving a name we give identity to a child for other people not for God. All parents want their child to be seen separately with a unique identity in the world. They want all these things for when their child grows up, but God wants all these things right from the beginning of our life. From this, you can know how much God loves us and our children. How much He is concerned for us. He loves our children more than we love them. This is why He calls them His children (Ezekiel 16:21). He considers our children as His children and He has given them to us to take care of them. So his love and plans for us and our children are far high than we think or imagine. So being a caretaker of God's children means we need to give them good spiritual food from their early childhood, and the bride said she is ready for this task.

The bride said, *"I was in his eyes like one who found peace"*. In some translations, instead of "peace", the word "contentment" is used. So bride introduces herself as someone who brings contentment to the bridegroom. When the bride decided to take care of the new believers and children in the church, she was satisfied that she is a wife who brings contentment to her husband. In a marital relationship, it is necessary that the husband and wife bring contentment to each other. When there is no contentment in this relationship, it will fall apart and result in separation or divorce. We should know each other. We should know what things please my partner and what things bring strife. The bride knew that if believers will take care of other believers and behave like a wall then these things will please the Lord. Believers need to be like a wall that can stop the world entering the church. Believers need to go into the world to preach the gospel but we should take care that world does not come into the church and pollute it.

8:11

Solomon had a vineyard at Baal Hamon. He leased out the vineyard to keepers. Each was to bring a thousand shekels of silver for its fruit.

Usually, we think that David was just a shepherd who became a king, but the Bible tells us that David was also a good administrator. He had many servants. A list of his officers is given in 1-Chronicles 27. Along with others, he had officers to manage his vineyards. His son Solomon expanded his father's work. Solomon had a big network of labourers. He sent thousands of people to neighbouring countries as labourers. Ten thousand labourers were working in Lebanon to cut the wood (1-Kings 5:14). There were several other workers in different fields.

Solomon rented his vineyard to his servants to work. Each one of them had to pay a thousand pieces of silver. In Song of Songs, Solomon represents Jesus. In Matthew 21, Jesus told us the parable of the vineyard. According to Isaiah 5:7, *"For the vineyard of Yahweh of Armies is the house of Israel"*. Tenants are the leaders God appointed in Israel. These leaders could be prophets, judges, and kings. They had to work in the vineyard, use the fruit for their own good but they had to pay for using the land and its fruit.

Everyone whom God appointed in his field/ vineyard has also been provided for from the same vineyard and field. For example, God commanded the Israelites to pay taxes to the king for his support. In 1-Samuel 8:11-18, God commanded the Israelites to pay a tenth of the produce of the land and livestock to the king. God also commanded in Deuteronomy 17:15, *"you shall surely set him whom Yahweh your God chooses as king over yourselves"*. So the kings were chosen by God and their rights to get taxes were also determined by God. In this way, kings were the appointed servants of God and their wages were also decided by God. Being appointed servants in the vineyard of God, kings are the tenants charged to take care of the vineyard, which is Israel. They have to pay to the owner of the vineyard (God) a thousand pieces of silver as a tribute. God doesn't need silver or gold. Bringing silver into God's presence shows that they will save souls for His glory's sake. A king maintains law and order in the land. In the reign of a good king, people live peaceably and give thanks to the Lord. The thanksgiving of people is like a thousand pieces of silver in God's presence.

Each one of the vineyard tenants had to pay a thousand shekels or coins of silver. It means there was more than one tenant in the vineyard, which is Israel. The three main tenants in Israel were: prophets, kings, and priests. We have seen that kings were allowed to get taxes from people. In the same way, God ordered the Israelites to take care of priests and Levites. Numbers 18:8-9 talks about the portion for priests and Numbers 18:25-26 talks about the share of the Levities.

Numbers 18:8-9

Yahweh spoke to Aaron, "Behold, I myself have given you the command of my wave offerings, even all the holy things of the children of Israel. I have given them to you by reason of the anointing, and to your sons, as a portion forever. This shall be yours of the most holy things from the fire: every offering of theirs, even every meal offering of theirs, and every sin offering of theirs, and every trespass offering of theirs, which they shall render to me, shall be most holy for you and for your sons.

Numbers 18:25-26

Yahweh spoke to Moses, saying, "Moreover you shall speak to the Levites, and tell them, 'When you take of the children of Israel the tithe which I have given you from them for your inheritance, then you shall offer up a wave offering of it for Yahweh, a tithe of the tithe."

Here we see that priests and Levities are the appointed servants of God in the Old Testament. People used to bring offerings before

God. Those offerings were given to priests and levities as a gift for their service to God and men. We can say that they were paid by God to work in His vineyard. Being paid workers themselves, they had to bring something to God as a product of their service. God wanted this payment in the form of silver which is the salvation of His people. In the New Testament instead of three, we see five tenants in Ephesians 4:11-12, "*He gave some to be apostles; and some, prophets; and some, evangelists; and some, shepherds and teachers; for the perfecting of the saints, to the work of serving, to the building up of the body of Christ*". No matter whoever serves in God's vineyard, His demand is the same from everyone: a thousand pieces of silver which is the salvation of people.

8:12

My own vineyard is before me. The thousand are for you, Solomon, two hundred for those who tend its fruit.

In the previous verse, we learned about the tenants who were working in Solomon's vineyard. In this verse, we will learn about the bride's vineyard. In the previous verse, each tenant had to pay a thousand shekels of silver to Solomon but in this verse, the bride is offering the same amount of silver to Solomon. First, it was Solomon who hired the servants. Now it is the bride who hired the servants. Solomon was running his business on the basis of a contract that tenants would keep the fruit and pay to Solomon in the form of silver. On the contrary to Solomon's method, the bride hired the servants and paid them their salaries. So in this case bride will have the fruit, not the tenants.

Every verse of the Bible can teach us different lessons. From Song of Songs 8:11-12, we can see the two eras of the Old and New Testaments. Verse 11 represents the Old Testament and verse 12 represents the New Testament. In the Old Testament, God appointed the tenants. Isaiah 5:7 tells us that Israel is the vineyard of God and Israel is God's bride. After the resurrection of Christ, Jesus sent His disciples into the whole world to bring everyone to salvation (Matthew 28:19-20). Jesus gave the responsibility to the Church to bring everyone of the world to the saving grace of Christ. So the world is the vineyard where the church has to work and the church is the bride of Christ. Therefore, the church appoints workers in the vineyard (Ephesians 4:11). As it was the duty of the Israelites to take care of the needs of people serving God; in the same way now it is the duty of the church to take care of the appointed servants of Christ. As it is the church's duty, therefore, we see in Song of Songs 8: 12 the bride is paying the workers in the vineyard. But the same amount which we see that tenants paying to Solomon, the bride is also paying the bridegroom. It means whether we look at Old Testament saints or New Testament saints when we come before God, He has the same question for us, "How fruitful were we when we were in the world?" Sometimes we think that in the Old Testament God was only concerned with the Israelites, but right from the beginning He introduced Himself as God of the nations. When He blessed Abraham, He said that you would be the father of nations (Genesis 12:1-4, 17:4-5). When the Israelites came out of Egypt, it was not only the Israelites who came out of Egypt; there were many non-Israelites who came out with them. The gentiles who came out with the Israelites were accepted by God and mentioned as "a mix multitude" or "other people".

Exodus 12:37-38

"The children of Israel traveled from Rameses to Succoth, about six hundred thousand on foot who were men, in addition to children. A mixed multitude went up also with them, with flocks, herds, and even very much livestock."

Moses saved not only Israelites but gentiles as well. When Jesus sent His disciples to win the world for Christ, Peter was the first one through whom gentiles accepted Christ (Acts chapter 10). In this way, whether it was the Old Testament or New Testament, God's prime target is to save people; this thing we see in the form of payment which is made to Jesus. The amount, which is a thousand pieces of silver, is the same in both testaments; which shows God's heart for the lost souls.

8:13

You who dwell in the gardens, with friends in attendance, let me hear your voice!

When we read Song of Songs Chapter 5, we see that bride was living in the city but the bridegroom's heart was with His garden. He wanted to spend His time in His orchard, taking care of the fruitful plants and trees. In chapter 5, she didn't care much when the bridegroom was knocking on the door. So the bridegroom left the place and went to his orchard (Song of Songs 6:1-3). In the last chapter, we are seeing that their relationship is quite mature now. She understands that she needs to live with her husband, where her husband desires to keep a watch over the plants of the garden. Now she is living in the garden, preferring the choices of her husband. Our security is hidden in preferring the choices of Jesus. When the bride ignored this fact in chapter 5, she went into trouble. She misbehaved and was beaten by the city guards. Now she knows that her husband, Jesus, is her protector and well-wisher; so she seems happy in the place where the husband wanted to be.

In Asian culture, in ancient times, young couples were not allowed to express their feelings openly, especially if they were unmarried. A girl or boy used to share their heart only with close and confident friends, so that their love affair or attraction may not be revealed to others. Now the friends of the boy used to convey his message to the girl, and the girl's friends used to tell the girl's message to the boy. It was their desire that the girl and the boy may meet each other and share their feelings with each other. The same kind of love and desire is expressed by the bridegroom that I want to be direct in contact with you without anyone in between us.

If we have something to tell Christ, we don't need any messenger in between us. We need to go confidently in His presence. *"In him we have boldness and access in confidence through our faith in him"* (Ephesians 3:12). We know He is ready to listen to us. "*This is the boldness which we have toward him, that if we ask anything according to his will, he listens to us. And if we know that he listens to us, whatever we ask, we know that we have the petitions which we have asked of him*" (1-John 5:14-15). We have confidence in Him that we can ask anything we need from Him. Kings, queens, presidents, and other officers may have their limitations but God is unlimited. No matter how powerful a king is, he can't roll back the sun (2-Kings 20:11). Joshua and Isaiah prayed confidently for the sun to move (Joshua 10:12-13) and God did according to their request. This miraculous movement was attested to by secular historians of the period. No one has the power to stop or send the rain but Elijah requested it of God and He did it (James 5:17-18). He wants to build our confidence so that we can raise our voices to fulfil our needs.

Sometimes we become so busy in our ministry that we forget the One to whom we are ministering. We keep on serving Jesus, without coming in contact with Him. We become so busy in serving children in the orphanage, visiting people in hospitals, preparing sermons for meetings, or taking care of children in Sunday school that we forget to spend time alone with Jesus in prayer. When we become lazy in our prayer life, a time comes when we become so obsessed with our work or ministry that we stray far away from Jesus and our relationship becomes weaker day by day. When we serve others by sharing sermons or telling Bible stories to children, our listeners benefit. But, God doesn't only want others to listen to the Word from us; He also wants us to listen as well. He is waiting to listen to your voice. Spend time in prayer and then your ministry will be fruitful.

8:14

Come away, my beloved! Be like a gazelle or a young stag on the mountains of spices!

When we watch a gazelle or stag, we will notice that they are very fast in the mountains. They can go up and down the mountains briskly. This speed and their alertness sometimes save them from hunters and predators. The bride is longing for the bridegroom who is on the spice-laden mountains. Spices were of different kinds; some were used for a sweet smell; such spices were used in worship in the temple. Other spices were used for medicinal purposes.

Jesus went to heaven from the Mount of Olives (Acts 1:1-11). The Disciples worshiped Him there and came back in happiness with the hope of more spiritual blessings in the future. Spices do two things; the first one is to smell sweetly for worship and the second is to effect healing, which brings joy to the person who receives it. On the Mount of Olives, some similar kind of things happen; the disciples worshiped and were filled with joy.

Jesus went to heaven about two thousand years ago. Figuratively, He is sitting on the mountain of spices. Heaven is the mountain where He is staying now. When we pray, our help comes from heaven. The bride has been waiting for Christ to come back for two thousand years. We pray to Him to come soon and take us with Him.

Revelation 22:17

"The Spirit and the bride say, "Come!" He who hears, let him say, "Come!" He who is thirsty, let him come. He who desires, let him take the water of life freely."

It is the deep desire of the Holy Spirit that He wants to be with believers. On the other hand, the same cry can be observed among the believers, that they want to be with their creator. Although the

Holy Spirit wants Jesus to go and bring all the believers home, but something is holding Him back from coming again. The thing which is holding him back is the desire that many people could come to the saving grace of Christ; because He doesn't want anyone to perish. If we could feel, and take on, the responsibility that Jesus gave us while going to heaven that we may preach the gospel to everyone; then He will come soon. It is necessary that the Good News be preached to every nation before He comes. In this way, it is not Jesus who is delaying His coming. Our lack of interest in evangelism is the cause of any delay.

Printed in the United States
by Baker & Taylor Publisher Services